WE
are the
MUCH MORE!!!

Susie O'Berski
susie.oberski@gmail.com

xulon PRESS

Daily walk with His face and Jesus, smile + Shirle

DEDICATION

I dedicate this book to my parents, Les and Fran Hudson,
who so lovingly taught me Who Jesus is in word and deed;
Michigan Christian Campus Ministries,
who showed me how to better love and obey Him;
our marvelous five sons, John, Dan, Steve, Josh, and Matt,
who increased my prayer life ;)
with HIS SONshine;
and my loving, very wise husband, Michael,
who has encouraged my every step with
his faithful love and daily prayers!
To God be the glory!

BACKWARD

I know most books start with forwards but I am left handed and have always been backwards with many things so feel it is quite appropriate to start here. The real question in many of your minds is, "Why another book to add to the thousands upon thousands upon thousands that have never been read AND kill another tree?" Tree<u>s</u> if this turns out well! My answer is that it is my goal for 2010. Forever I have had people ask me about my goals and objectives for my life. I hate that question…I personally have always thought it was quite enough to breathe each breath and a marvelous gift to actually enjoy it and miraculous to survive it smiling! So I would answer with a wrinkled nose, "Umm, do I need more of a goal than to live whatever life God brings my way for His praise and glory?" That answer always threw people so they would ask me to be more specific and I would tell them, "God hasn't given me the specifics yet." That was always enough for me.

God has always been enough for me. More than enough! **MUCH MORE** than enough…that is what this book is all about.

TABLE OF CONTENTS

ACKNOWLEDGMENTS

The only way I have gotten this far in publishing this book is by God surrounding me with a tremendously supportive family and dear friends, my cheerleaders – thank you!

In addition, I had family and a few friends read along as I wrote and give me thumbs up or wrinkled noses, delivered with LOTS of love!

My wonderful sister, Kaye, retired (but tireless!) principal assisted me in the editing so that words were actually words – you are forever dear!

My very smart friend, Aline, painstakingly edited to help me appear to be smarter than I am – that is called a miracle, and I thank you!

The cover of the book is a copy of a gift painted by my treasured, adopted Mom and mentor, Mozell Huxtable, now home with our Lord and Savior.

My artistic consultant for the cover of the book, Eric Dush, gave me hours of his time without once complaining or changing his email address. Eric also added to the beauty of the cover by introducing me to his friend, Amy Gieschen, who amazingly drew the birds I wanted for the cover. They both generously shared their talents given so graciously by God – thank you! To see more of their work, you may go to their websites below:

Eric Dush – computer specialist: www.ericdush.com

Amy Lou Gieschen-Thill - landscape and figurative painter:

www.lifeandartintheup.blogspot.com and www.michiganlighthouseart.com

Despite Michael saying he did not want any more credit, he wonderfully gave up many, many of our normally shared hours together to see the completion of this book. All five sons and their wives cheered me on but I must say that Danny, Steve, and Matt were the most supportive in checking in to see how it was coming along and actually reading the book prior to publication. Because Steve does NOT like to read, John and Josh were probably praying for God to help him do it so they would not have to read it ☺ **My heart FULL of thanks and LOVE to ALL six of my favorite MEN!**

CHAPTER 1

WE are the MUCH MORE!!!

*"Therefore, I tell you, do not worry about your life,
what you will eat or drink; or about your body,
what you will wear. Is not life more important
than food, and the body more important than clothes?
Look at the birds of the air; they do not sow or reap or
store away in barns, and yet your Heavenly Father feeds
them. Are YOU not MUCH MORE valuable than they?"*
Matthew 6: 25,26

I think we live in a world where we are told we are to be the center of attention. The very title of this book and chapter would lead you to believe that I agree. My desire in the words that follow are to show you the complete opposite…that God is to be THE center of our attention…the center of ALL attention. As we come to focus on Him, to know His heart, to learn His ways, we shall find that His very creation is for us…not because of who we are, but because of WHOSE He wants us to be…His **MUCH MORE.**

I am a lover of His creation. It thrills me to watch Him working throughout each day; to see how He starts it off, carries it through, and closes it with the twinkling of the stars. What a delight to walk outside in His great wonder listening for the singing of the birds, His saying good morning with the breeze upon my cheeks, and to notice the colors He chooses for that day...just for me, just for you. God wants us to look at the fields along our varied roads and see His floral decorations strewed along the way. The branches of each tree raised in praise and dancing to the music of the winds He blows their way. Are our arms raised in praise? Are we dancing to the music of the winds He blows our way? We can be. We should be. He gave us breath of life to enjoy, to share with others, to point out His glory. We have a very personal God... do you know that? We do! Not only does he know the number of hairs on our head, our name by heart, our favorite AND least favorite things, but He WANTS us to know Him too. He wants us to open our eyes...we are **HIS** much more!

*"Why do we worry about clothes? See how the lilies of the field grow. They do not labor or spin. Yet I tell you that not even Solomon in all his splendor was dressed like one of these. If that is how God clothes the grass of the field, which is here today and tomorrow is thrown into the fire, will He not **MUCH MORE** clothe you, O you of little faith?"* Matthew 6:28-30

I love this! Even as I was typing that scripture, I started to put a question mark at the end of "see how the lilies of the field grow." But there is NO question mark. God is telling us to see; to see HIM in our daily happenings. This book began because I believe God has shared many wonderful things with me that He doesn't want me to hoard. Even now, He is reminding me this is HIS book, He wants to talk to you and me through it. He wants us to pay attention to His words. He wants us to pay attention to His world. He wants us to see Him in the world and dance!

*"So do not worry, saying, 'What shall we eat?' or 'What shall we drink?' or 'What shall we wear?' For the pagans run after all these things, and your Heavenly Father knows that you need them. But seek **first** His*

*kingdom and His righteousness, and **all** these things will be given to you as well. Therefore do not worry about tomorrow, for tomorrow will worry about itself. Each day has enough trouble of its own."* Matthew 6:31–34

God has been talking to us throughout creation. He gave us His written Word. He sent His Son. He has given us with His Holy Spirit to live within us and guide each step. When will we choose to listen? What does He say? **DO NOT WORRY! SEEK HIM FIRST! Seek HIS kingdom in your world** – and your world will look so different. Things that have always seemed so important will fade in importance because He has become #1. He not only will take care of today, but all of your tomorrows. Why? Because **WE are His MUCH MORE!!!**

CHAPTER 2

START

I have always wanted to write a book. Is that an unusual desire to have for a child growing up? I don't think so. Guess what, I am related to Mark Twain! Really! I am even pretty good at painting fences. Not really. Who? His real name was Samuel Clemens and better known for his writings of Tom Sawyer and Huckleberry Finn. Anyway, Mark Twain IS my 5th cousin on my Mom's side and my Grandma Johnson always used to talk proudly about Mark Twain. Although only getting as far as the 8th grade, Grandma was also a writer. While I was at Michigan State University (Go Green!) she weekly wrote beautifully descriptive letters where her words came alive; I could picture the birds outside her window chatting away with various "conversations."

We also grew up having lots of books around so I treasure books and love to read. Nancy Drew and Trixie Belden mysteries were my favorites. I used to go on bike rides (we lived out in the country) and explore the back fields with my brother, Scott, dreaming up different story lines. I even had a pen name…Cookie Darnell. Seeing as I never did anything with the few pages I wrote, Cookie is no more known than Susie O'Berski.

This is where my Dad comes in. You would have loved him, my hero! Tall, dark, and very handsome, he was the kind of father every girl loved to show off to her friends, introduce to her teachers, have walk her down the aisle…ok, it was really a grassy slope in our back yard. I delighted in seeing all five of our sons fall in love with him as Grandpa, watching him play, converse, direct and love them back completely. He was such a man of order, action and fun! No one knew how to work or play harder than my Dad.

Dad grew up in the depression with six siblings, three older, three younger. My Grandpa Hudson worked for the railroad in Pontiac, Michigan and was killed by being crushed by a train when my Dad was 17. My Grandma was a God-fearing woman and raised those kids to trust and rely on the Lord. As a natural leader, I think it was then Dad jumped into position of overseer for the family. The older and younger siblings all looked to my Dad. My Grandma did a marvelous job of teaching them the importance of family and I think amidst the sadness of Grandpa's death, my Dad learned to take his eyes off of himself and think of others. No time for selfishness, mouths had to be fed and rent had to be paid.

Upon graduation, Dad headed off for college at the University of Michigan for law school. World War II had begun and he completed one semester. Again, no time for selfishness, he quit school to enlist in the Army. He and Mom got married in the middle of the war and our family began upon his return; Kaye, Scott, me, and Patti. His love for family and Mom's love for God served to build strong roots in us; roots that reach deep into God's never-ending streams of water, refreshment for life.

*"Blessed is the man who does not walk in the counsel of the wicked or stand in the way of sinners or sit in the seat of mockers. But his delight is in the law of the Lord, and on His law he meditates day and night. He is like a tree planted by **streams of water**, which yields its fruit in season and whose leaf does not wither. Whatever he does prospers." Psalms 1:1–3*

Indeed, God yielded fruit in my Dad's many seasons of life and (almost) whatever he did prospered. As much as my Dad worked and "prospered," he would be quick to say it was NOT about money. He enjoyed his work and the people he met. He was fueled by the challenge of business and once he became involved with commercial real estate said it was more like a hobby than work because it was so much fun! He was a visionary and could see what needed to be where on which piece of property, when the right time was, and who to go after as the best entrepreneur. He and Mom owned and ran countless small businesses successfully (grocery store, drug store, hardware store, real estate broker), and Dad invested himself in politics locally and statewide. The family man that Dad was, he did not run for a second term as State Representative…he missed being home with his family too much. He would be the first to say that he DID prosper in whatever he did – he just did not always make money!

MUCH of my parent's teaching was about character, being a good, kind person, and being able to look yourself in the mirror at night and sleep peacefully. They had strong work ethics. Dad was king of getting us to work and make it into a game; raking leaves, picking up acorns, mowing the lawn, whatever it took to make a house a home.

MUCH MORE of their teaching was about the importance of God and family as priority in life. It takes time and effort to make a good family by investing in one another, and to do so you had to say no to some things so that you could say yes to family. Family meals together were important and Dad would close the store by 6 p.m. to be home for dinner. On Friday nights when the stores were open until 9:00 p.m. we would often meet him for a quick bite or he would run home to eat and then return to close the store. We always lived close to their businesses. Dad would often tell us to "make sure you build your nest warm" because you never know when you will need to gather in the chicks, and you want them to WANT to come home. We kids watched them care for their own parents, and in turn, we were able to care for our parents. We never questioned whether we would care for family – that was the definition of being family.

Don't get me wrong. Caring for family, though right, can be very hard. Toward the end of my Mom's life, she needed 24/7 care. Due to surgery for a mitral valve replacement, she shot a clot to her brain and had her initial stroke. In testing further, they found she had a brain aneurysm which doctors again surgically "fixed" only to have several strokes thereafter. We made one of the hardest decisions of our lives and handed our care of Mom over to a very special facility for Alzheimer and Dementia patients. They were good and we were still there with her but we almost felt like we had betrayed her because "they" weren't family. She would NEVER have said that, but we felt it nevertheless. Even though she did not always remember us, we remembered her – she was our Mom. Sounds silly I know but I hear many people say, as if it is okay, "Well, she/ he doesn't remember me anymore" to rationalize not going to visit. Sad. They are still FAMILY!

Up until then, Patti's family and our family took turns caring for her every other week for a year. We saw a very gentle side of our boys as they cared for and loved on their Grandma. I will forever love my husband (and I try to quickly remember this when I get mad at him) for allowing Mom to come and live with us. He was so kind to her. He protected her. He freed me to care for her. Scott would do his part, having stepped into the real estate business when my Dad died 12 years prior, visiting regularly, going on lunch outings, and taking her to visit family and friends. Kaye, working full time as principal of a large elementary school in Westport, Connecticut and having a family of her own, called Mom regularly and would fly out to visit as often as she could get away. Toward the last year, Kaye would come and reprieve us when we needed a break. It was a sacrifice for all of us but we gained so MUCH MORE than we ever gave up. Character was built in all of us that you cannot learn any other way.

You never had to ask my Dad how he did anything...he was pretty good about telling you! ☺ Not that he would brag on himself. That was not him. He was very good at teaching throughout life. He would grab any and every opportunity to teach us through all of life's little happenings…the good and the bad. Dad was a believer. He loved the Lord with every fiber of his body. Yet, he was not one to quote scripture or even pray great prayers aloud. He believed that it was our job to make the most of what God had given us and pass it onto our children and grandchildren…and he did.

> *"Love the Lord your God with **all** your heart and with **all** your soul and with **all** your strength. These commandments that I give you today are to be upon your hearts. **Impress them on your children**. Talk about them when you sit at home and when you walk along the road, when you lie down and when you get up. Tie them as symbols on your hands and bind them on your foreheads. Write them on the doorframes of your houses and on your gates." Deuteronomy 6:5–9*

The quote he liked the best for me was "a fool and his money soon parts." I couldn't argue with him because as soon as I would get any money, I would want to spend it. I was very good at losing money at the county fairs with the ring toss. I thought for sure I would surely beat the odds and win that big stuffed animal. So dime after hard-earned dime was thrown away. Dad didn't stop me. He warned me, letting me see and then learn the consequences of my actions…poverty! As much as I grew tired of hearing that, rarely do I think of buying anything without asking myself if I really need it. I have come to realize most things are wants. This was NOT to teach us to hoard our money. Dad was one of the most generous people I have ever known. He often would meet someone through his business who needed something and he and Mom would make sure they received it. I cannot count how many burial plots they bought for others when a family member would die. Who thinks to buy burial plots? Someone who thinks outside the box to meet needs. He taught us to work and SAVE money so that we would have it to give away when God directed. I love that! Much of this thinking has helped us be debt free today, free to give away God's money when it is needed for others. You cannot buy that kind of joy!

S T A R T. Where did that come from? Every breath of my Dad's life. All of us kids got sick of hearing him spell it out for us…**S T A R T**. With each spelling came a teaching on life; an example for us to see more clearly that nothing ever gets accomplished until it is begun. For me, the beginning part has always been the hardest. Once I would start anything, it never seemed as bad as I had made it up to be. Even my Mom would tell us to "Never put off until tomorrow what you can do today." She would remind us we are not guaranteed any more "extra" time tomorrow and you never know what tomorrow will bring. Given, to sit on the couch to "just relax" is sometimes difficult to me if I have left things undone. To **START** and not put off is the only way they achieved anything. That is the only way we would achieve anything.

So simple, but so true. I did not say easy. It takes thought, and "want to" and action and more action and **MUCH MORE** action and follow through. This is not leaving God out of the picture – He **IS** the picture. HE is the reason for doing every-thing! Our purpose! Our life! **HE IS SO MUCH MORE!!!**

P. S. Get this! Mark Twain wrote, "The secret of getting ahead is getting **START**ed. The secret of getting **START**ed is breaking your complex, overwhelming tasks into small, manageable tasks, and then **START**ing on the first one."

CHAPTER 3

CHOOSING FAITH

A good place to START would be to tell you how I came to be a lover of Jesus. My Mom. As great as my Dad was, my Mom was the one who demonstrated Jesus to me day in and day out. She had unfaltering poise. My Dad was much more the emotional one who added the excitement into our lives with his varying businesses and adventurous spirit. Mom was our balance. Maybe that was the Johnson side of her from Grandpa Johnson; rarely highs or lows but dependability you could count on.

My Mom did not grow up in a Christian home. She saw Jesus in her Uncle Shirley (a good Southern name for a man – eek!) and Aunt Ellen and asked if she could go to church with them. When she was a little older she would walk to church on her own and got involved in their youth group. It was not until my grandparent's last years that they became Christians. Why? It was because of my Mom's consistent love and Godly lifestyle. Mom knew what she wanted and would hold onto it once she obtained it. Strong. but so meek. I have heard a definition of meekness that fits my Mom, "Strength under control." She always knew Who was in control.

Throughout our growing up years at home, Mom would see us through whatever the day would bring. Her life verse was one she often would quote to us. Kaye, Scott, Patti and

I all utilize it in our lives today. Psalms 118:24 says, "This is the day the Lord has made, let us rejoice and be glad in it." She reminded us it was a choice – *let us* rejoice. No moaning and groaning for her, nor for us! We needed to **CHOOSE** to recognize the day as God's day and be thankful for it. It is so MUCH about an **attitude of gratitude.**

Not only would Mom help Dad with his many businesses, but she would engineer each of our happenings with smooth expertise. She was tireless. She NEVER complained about her unending chores and was faster than anyone in doing them. She was untouched by our childhood catastrophes. Oh, she would respond with immediate kindness and caring kisses on our boo boos, but remained unrattled. Nothing ever seemed to "Rock her boat." We learned early it was because she knew the Captain of the ship.

It is funny what you remember about your childhood. I vividly recall the day I decided I wanted to be just like my Mom. I was about eight years old. It was a summer day and we had come inside to cool off. Mom was ironing all our clothes and Scott ran inside, slamming the door, and the iron fell. Scared, we jumped and thought she would be upset that he had made the iron fall. Nope. Instead, she thanked the Lord right away for protecting all of us from getting burned and keeping the iron intact. No punishment for Scott. She understood her children and knew he had not meant any harm. She explained it was an accident, something that happened without intention, and to be taken in stride as part of life. My favorite part? She thanked the Lord for His protection from the iron not burning any of us. She thanked the Lord...for an accident!! Such wisdom. I wanted **MORE** of what she had...**Jesus**!

When I was 19, Dad had his first heart attack. We were getting ready to go my cousin Darrell's wedding, and Dad was not feeling well. He was not a complainer so when he said he was not feeling well, you knew he had to be sick. He did not want to spoil the evening (!!!) so he told us to go ahead to the wedding. He had Mom take him to the hospital. Mom calmly saw us off to the wedding and assured us Dad would be okay, as he was in God's hands. She also reminded us to pray for Dad but to not take away from the excitement of the wedding for the others. Mom was never an attention grabber and always thought of others first. Again, her calmness stood out to me. In fact, after Mom had Dad all settled at the hospital (yes, he had a heart attack), Dad insisted Mom go to the reception so no one would be worried. They were an amazing team! I later asked Mom how she had stayed so calm. Simply put, she said, "Honey, you either believe or you don't."

Faith had come easily for me. From birth on, I had heard of and seen God working in our lives. We always went to Sunday School and Church every Sunday. We would occasionally go to a good 'ole fashioned tent meeting and hear the preaching of a traveling evangelist. Our church would call them a "REVIVAL" and I could see why – those preachers could shout loud enough the raise the dead! I actually like loud, passionate preaching BUT if a church if alive and well, why do they need reviving? Hmmm. We even went to Wednesday night services if a "good" missionary was going to be there but came to believe that was why most of them were sent overseas…nobody else wanted them! I want you to know I know better now but, sad to say, that is what I use to think of missionaries.

I say all of that to let you know our church was great at the basics…how to get saved. However, I never saw them having any fun with life and I believed if Jesus was Who He said He was, life had to be great! So when I went to college at Michigan State University (Go Green!), I sought out different churches to find the joy that I thought must go along with Jesus. I faithfully went every Sunday. It was not until the middle of my senior year that I finally agreed to go with some friends to His House, a Christian campus ministry. Not only did they teach the basics but they made the rest of Scripture come alive – with JOY! I was challenged to live like Jesus so others could see Him!

One of my all time favorite books is <u>Faith Is Not A Feeling</u> by Ney Bailey. Throughout it she declares how we cannot base our life on feelings, they will change. We all know feelings can be like a rollercoaster. Instead, we choose to believe in the unchanging, One and Only, God. We choose to believe that His "Word is truer than anything we are feeling or experiencing right now" (pg. 5). God is REALITY, not our feelings. One of my favorite scriptures comes from the FAITH chapter and is about Moses in Hebrews 11:25–27:

> *"He **CHOSE** to be mistreated along with the people of God rather than to enjoy the pleasures of sin for a short time. He regarded disgrace for the sake of Christ as of greater value than the treasures of Egypt, because he was looking ahead to his reward (JESUS). By faith he left Egypt, not fearing the king's anger; **he persevered because he saw HIM Who is invisible**."*

He persevered **BECAUSE he saw HIM Who is INVISIBLE**! Invisible!!! Faith goes where eyes can't see. It has been said that our faith is only as strong as the object of our faith. **JESUS**. Our faith is NOT in feelings; our faith comes because we **CHOOSE** to believe that Jesus, and all He claims to be through His Word, is Truth. Hebrews 11:1 says, "Faith is being sure of what we hope for and certain of what we do not see." How can invisible be reality? Because it is faith in a very certain God. God IS reality.

I went through a very difficult time in my life when we moved from my very favorite home, neighborhood, friends, and church in Brighton, Michigan to Mt. Pleasant. It was not Mt. Pleasant that was the problem, it was me. With every fiber of my body, I believed we were to make the move so Michael could be Campus Minister at Central Michigan University. I did not want to leave. I did not want to give up all I had. Brighton was a perfect driving distance to our parents; mine in Pontiac and Michael's in Grosse Pointe Farms. We had four of our five boys by that time and they had friends. But it really wasn't about them, it was about me. I knew Michael would get involved in ministry (as he should and as I knew he needed to do) and life would go on for him. But back to me – what about MY life?!!! As MUCH as I knew we were to be there, I did not want to be and fought it for the first year. Before Michael would go to work in the morning, I would go out walking in our neighborhood and cry out to God, "WHY?" Pretty much back to "me" over and over and over again. Finally, after a full year (sad to say) I heard God talking to me, and of course reminding me, that, "Susan, it is not about you." (God always calls me Susan when He needs me to listen.)

God gently reviewed that my surrender to Him gave Him the right to do with my life whatever He needed...I told Him I meant it BUT I had NO idea that would mean me not having what I wanted...after all, I always had, so why would things change now?! I reminded God (like He needed that) that we have four active little boys and Michael was too busy and I needed him to be there for me; I needed my parents and friends to be there for me; and I wanted my old church back! Guess what God said? He directed my eyes and my soul to Psalms 62:1, 2, 5 – 8:

> *"My soul finds rest **in God alone**; my salvation comes from **Him**. **He alone** is my **Rock**, my **Salvation**; **He** is my **Fortress**, I will never be shaken (yeah, right!)... Find rest, O my soul, **in God alone**; my **hope** comes from Him. **He alone** is my **Rock** and my **Salvation**; **He** is my **Fortress**, I will not be shaken. (ok, maybe) My salvation and my honor depend on **God**; **He** is my mighty **Rock**, my **Refuge**. Trust in **Him** at **ALL** times, O people; Pour out your heart to **Him**, for **God is our Refuge**."*

Wow! I got it!!! God's patient, loving kindness had gotten through to me. It was not about me. I could not put my hope in anyone but God to meet MY needs, MY wants, MY expectations. They would fail me. Not because they were bad or wrong but because **ONLY GOD** would never fail me. **ONLY GOD** could be my hope...not Michael, or the boys, or my family, or my friends, or any church, or any house, or any job, or good health. **ONLY GOD**. Ney Bailey says, "God is the only 'constant' in life, and everything else is variable…If we put our hopes in variables, we'll invariably be disappointed (pg. 59)… my will is the key. With my will I could choose to believe God and choose to take Him at His Word regardless of what my feelings told me" (pg. 71).

At that moment, life became better in Mt. Pleasant. Not because life in Mt. Pleasant had changed. I had changed. I had chosen, with my will, to put my faith in **Jesus**, my **ONLY** constant, and not my feelings. **Faith is not a feeling, it is a choice**.

Declaration of Faith

I choose
To believe
*That **God Himself***
And what He chooses to provide
At this moment
Is all I need.

I am complete in Christ
Colossians 2:10

(by Verna Berkey)

CHAPTER 4

REMEMBER

"Remember this, fix it in mind, take it to heart,
you rebels.
Remember the former things, those of long ago;
I am God and there is no other;
I am God, and there is none like me.
I make known the end from the beginning,
from ancient times, what is still to come.
I say: My purpose will stand, and I will do what I please.
From the east I summon a bird of prey; from a far-off
land, a man to fulfill my purpose. What I have said,
that will I bring about;
What I have planned, that will I do."
Isaiah 46: 8 - 11

It is not that we forget. We fail to remember. God knows that. God also knows our need to remember and tells us repeatedly throughout the Bible to remember. He knows when life is going good, our mind tends to be on our self. He knows when life is not going so good, our mind tends to be on our self. He knows we are a self-centered people. He knows us so well He wants to help us refocus on Him, the One worth focusing on. He wants us to remember He is mine and I am His. God doesn't care who we know, He wants us to know Whose we are.

I majored in Social Work and Psychology at MSU...have I said "Go Green?" During the summers was blessed to work in the Juvenile Court Division of Oakland County. Not only was I allowed to have my own case load of delinquents, but I was able to take their cases to court...supervised, of course. There were days when I would have eight cases to prepare and represent in court and I would panic and moan and groan to my Mom and she would wisely remind me to "remember." Remember that I had panicked with exams and had come out okay. Next time I had eleven cases in court. I panicked, I even prayed, and then I remembered how God had never failed me. Once I was married and was pregnant, having our first son, John, I again panicked. "What have I done? What am I doing?! How will I know how to parent this baby??!!" I again prayed. Then I remembered all those exams in school, the eleven court cases I had survived, and panicked again – I'm having a baby!!! Not a silly 'ole case! Again God reminded me He had taken me through the past 26 years and He would not leave me now. I love the following verse:

"Never will I leave you, never will I forsake you."
Hebrews 13: 5

In Greek, it actually means never, no never, no never! God says He will **NEVER** leave us. That is something worth remembering! Our additional sons # 2, 3, 4, and 5 came along with the same Helper. Granted, I seemed to forget during some lapses of labor and my husband's hair is gray now due to my "lack" of calmness, but at least he still has hair - I didn't pull it out!

I am quite simple. In fact, my sweet brother, Scott, had a sweatshirt made up for me with "UNCOMPLICATED" on it as a joke but I really liked it. I still own it. It reminds me of the need for doing whatever it takes to remember God, whether others think I am silly or not; simple or not. I purpose to surround myself with things that constantly remind me of who I am and Whose I am. In our great room over the fire place we have a large picture with deer grazing by a still lake surrounded by mountains. Michael and I have our quiet time in there every morning and instantly when I look upon that picture I am reminded of our Creator and the beauty of His creation...and I praise Him. I am stilled by the quiet lake and remember Isaiah 46:10, "Be still and know that I am God." I will often meditate on that verse, one of many I used during the births of our sons.

Under the picture, on the mantle, is one of my favorite Christmas cards that we have had framed. It simply says, **BELIEVE**, with the nativity scene in the background and the star brightly shining over the manger. Under **BELIEVE** it says, **Believe the Promise, Share the Hope, Live the Joy!** My goal. I have to remember in order to do it – so I have a constant reminder in front of me daily.

We have a beautiful glass hutch my parents had specially made for our family cabin. When we sold the cabin, we inherited the hutch. In it we have various bird plates and carved birds reminding me over and over of how much God cares for the birds, but how He cares **SO MUCH MORE** for you and me! Because I am so simple and forgetful, I ask God to remind me Who He is. On our daily walks I am reminded of Who is in charge as I look at all His beauty around me. Remembering HE is in charge, and I am not, I quickly surrender the throne I too often try to take over – I need these reminders.

I need help as I go into my day remembering whatever comes into the day is there ONLY because God has allowed it...and it doesn't knock Him off His throne – He is more than able to handle it! I ask God for His perspective on the day. I listen for His birds singing His praise, knowing if they can sing to Him, **SO MUCH MORE** should I sing His praise. Often when I am struggling with something, I ask God for a reminder of His love and so many, many times He sends a bird to fly in front of me. He wants us to know Him. He wants us to ask Him. God delights in our wanting Him active in our lives.

All Promises Kept. Pretty simple. Pretty significant. I want a God Who keeps His promises.

Also in our office is another favorite gift from Melissa Hayes from our church here in Kalamazoo, Oakland Drive Christian Church. Melissa made it for her beloved Grandma in 2000. She most graciously has given it to me because she knows I love bears. We are THE O'BEARski's! It is a needlepoint of an angel bear with a rainbow and the words, EXPECT A MIRACLE. Miracles are all around us, simply look in the face of a child or senior saint. We just have to open our eyes and heart to see miracles.

I have a house filled with things that invoke memories. There are priceless pictures of our children and grandchildren all over with smiles that melt my heart. They remind me of my many blessings. Pictures of my "born into" family and "married into" family and they remind me to be thankful. I have an old clown doll, Lumpy, who is best "friends" with my sister Patti's clown doll, Bunky, and they were made and given to us by Zelda and Bob Grant, our life long family friends. Lumpy reminds me to smile and have fun, to NOT take myself too seriously. Why is it we take ourselves so seriously but don't take God seriously enough?

A favorite pillow says, "REAL LOVE STORIES NEVER HAVE ENDINGS." It reminds me that God's love never ends and I am committed to my marriage for the long haul. NO options. Feelings come and go but love is a choice and I have chosen Michael...for whom I am ever grateful! We also have a heart-shaped plaque in our bathroom that says, "Choose Thy Love, Love Thy Choice." Good reminder.

Sometimes I don't want to think of others. Sometimes I don't want to serve. Sooooo, I have a serving tray in our kitchen from one of my very dearest friends, Linda Hanniford. It reminds me of Joshua 24:15, "Choose for yourselves (SUSAN) this day whom you will serve...but as for me and my household, we will serve the Lord." I am called back to the choice I made years ago...YOU lead Lord, I will follow and serve YOU.

I am the Queen of being late. I KNOW it is wrong and continue to strive to be on time; NOT putting myself before others. I LOVE to be in charge. Our dear friends, Kevin and Deb Leahy gave us a little framed clock without any hands that says, "May the time of our family always be set by God's loving hand." I am lovingly reminded, again, He is in charge and I am not. It also strongly reminds me I surrendered my all to God years ago, including everything and anything I do with my time, and it is HIS.

Another framed card with a saying by Emerson is "All I have seen teaches me to trust the Creator for all I have not seen." A little plate with the word LIFE in the middle is surrounded by "Live Well, Laugh Often, Love Much"…we have another pillow with that same saying. Sometimes I need to be reminded more than once. That is why I ask God to remind me over and over again that **I am His MUCH MORE**…**WE are His SO MUCH MORE!**

CHAPTER 5

EYES TO SEE

Be Thou my Vision, O Lord of my heart;
Naught be all else to me, save that Thou art.
Thou my best Thought, by day or by night,
waking or sleeping, Thy presence my Light.

Be Thou my Wisdom, and Thou my true Word;
I ever with Thee and Thou with me, Lord;
Thou my great Father, I Thy true son;
Thou in me dwelling, and I with Thee one.

Be Thou my battle Shield, Sword for the fight;
Be Thou my Dignity, Thou my Delight;
Thou my soul's Shelter, Thou my high Tower:
Raise Thou me heavenward, O Power of my power.

Riches I heed not, nor man's empty praise,
Thou mine Inheritance, now and always:
Thou and Thou only, first in my heart,

High King of Heaven, my Treasure Thou art.
High King of Heaven, my victory won,
May I reach Heaven's joys, O Bright Heaven's Son!

Heart of my own heart, whatever befall,
Still be my Vision, O Ruler of all.
(Versed by Eleanor Hull, 1912, Copyright: Public Domain)

B E THOU MY VISION was one song our son, Danny, and his wife, Kristin, chose for their wedding. I have sung it a hundred times, but it filled my heart anew the day they gave their lives to each other. That day they asked God, in front of all those witnesses, to help them keep their eyes focused on Him.

Eyes to see. Doesn't that seem a little redundant? Yet God warns us in Isaiah 6: 9, 10 and Jesus in Matthew 13:14–16, "You will be ever hearing but never understanding; you will be ever seeing but never perceiving. For this people's heart has become calloused; they hardly hear with their ears, and they have closed their eyes. Otherwise they might see with their eyes, hear with their ears, understand with their hearts and turn, and I would heal them." Ouch! How sadly true that we are ever seeking after more and more knowledge, yet missing God.

Years ago we lived in Brighton, Michigan, and commuted back and forth to Ann Arbor where Michael was a campus minister on the University of Michigan's campus. For a long period of time there was a sign along the expressway adver-tising the University of Michigan Hospital and it simply said, KNOWLEDGE HEALS. Simply wrong! Every time I saw the sign I would say to myself, or any of the boys who were with me, "Nuh uh, God heals." For sure, God gives us wisdom to heal but there is a vast difference between knowledge healing and God healing. Even Solomon in all of his wisdom knew the vanity of knowledge without God is like chasing after the wind. (Ecclesiastes 6:9) I know we live in a world of higher educa-tion. More. Masters. Doctorates. Second doctorates. Why do we continue to chase after more knowledge? More pleasure? More advancement in our jobs? More riches? We quest to fill a void only God can fill.

God is the One Who has created the world and everything in it and yet we fail to go to Him. He, indeed, can and wants to use this knowledge to bring healing, pleasure, and wholeness to His creation. But as Creator, He knows life without Him is empty. Without Him, we are blinded. Satan knows that too and is in a spiritual battle all of the time with THE God. "The god of this age (Satan) has blinded the minds of unbelievers, so that they cannot SEE the light of the gospel of the glory of Christ, Who is the image of God" (II Corinthians 4: 4).

What surprises me and breaks my heart are the believers who allow Satan to turn their eyes away from the Truth – to CHOOSE to turn their eyes away from THE Truth. Satan may tempt us, but ultimately, WE CHOOSE. Turn to Him and He gives you not just eyes, but sight. "Blessed are your eyes because they see, and your ears because they hear" (Matthew 13:16). God is ready. God is waiting. God is wanting us to finally realize we need help, we need the Helper. Who better to ask than the One Who knows us best, Our Creator?

*"**Ask** and it will be given to you; **seek** and you will find ;**knock** and the door will be opened to you. For **everyone** who asks receives; he who seeks finds; and to him who knocks, the door will be opened. Which of you, if his son asks for bread, will give him a stone? Or if he asks for a fish, will give him a snake? If you, then, though you are evil, know how to give good gifts to your children, how **MUCH MORE** will your Father in Heaven give good gifts to those who ask Him!" Matthew 7: 7-12*

Much of my thinking on this comes from having been there, done that. Having been raised in a Christian family, I came to know OF Jesus early. I came to KNOW Him later. At a certain point I realized I had a critical spirit. Ugly. People probably thought I was a nice person. God showed me how sad my superior way of thinking made Him…and that came to break my heart. I am not sure it was until we had our own children that I realized how much I had hurt God by thinking little of some of His children. It was not the ugly prejudice of skin color or nationality. My parents did an amazing job on teaching us the value of all people. However, I missed their point of "all" people. My prejudice was much worse. I would "see" those inferior who: did not believe the same, did not worship the same, had less education, did not have good work ethics, were beggars, parented poorly, dressed differently, colored and wore their hair differently, and lacked "proper" care of their body by overeating or under exercising. By "seeing" others as inferior, I "saw" myself as superior. My own "god" on my throne dictating right and wrong, thinking how righteous I was, breaking God's heart.

Having been in campus ministry for years and church ministry even longer, we have been in many, many churches. I am not saying what church I was in when God first started shining His Light on my pitiful heart. I was doing my "dutiful" church pew sitting and thinking how awful the music was, how I wished they would learn to "do" it "right." Then they played a "good" song. I was so excited! It was about time! God turned my head so that I was gazing upon one of my dear little old lady friends. I knew her preference for music, and this was NOT it. I knew her love for God. She was worshiping the God she loved DESPITE the music. I was worshiping the music. From that moment on God has been changing my heart, my perspective. I cried out to Him for forgiveness and repented from my horrible superior attitude. I asked Him to cleanse me from my way of thinking and fill me with His way of thinking. I asked Him to help me SEE as He sees, to give me His perspective on things, on people, on life. I asked Him to help me love as He loves. He smiled and said okay.

Most often my "blind spots" have been revealed to me by God, not always so gently, but with great precision. Like a laser, He shines His Light on the area in my life I need to correct or eliminate, and cuts it out with His Sword. Again, not painless, but ever healing. It allows His Spirit to dwell freely as intended. Whenever I have not paid attention to God's "tap" on my shoulder, He has sent in the troops. Part of His marvelous provision in my life has been to surround me with strong family members and daring friends who have been willing to risk our relationship in order to hold me accountable to be God's woman. For that I will be forever thankful!

Do you have someone in your life who is willing to do the same for you? If you do not, pray for God to tell you who He knows would be His "eyes" here on earth for you, willing to pray for you and hold you accountable for His best. Are you willing to do that for someone else? Believe me, it is best if they ask you rather than you go up to them and tell them you are more than willing to "play" the Holy Spirit in their life and tell them whenever they are in the wrong!

Thankfully God is our Alpha and Omega, our Beginning and our End. Even better than that, HE IS our Forever and Always, our Constant, Ongoing, Ever Present God Who walks not only behind us, prepares our every tomorrow, but holds our hand through every present moment. Even though He has grown me by leaps and bounds, He knows I will still fail. I know I still fail. I know I need to seek Him first thing in the morning, throughout every day, and ask Him to close out my day. He is ever faithful.

I want you to know what He has done and what He is doing for me. My old prayer of "seeing" as He sees, has become one of many of my daily prayers. NOT because God has forgotten, but because I forget. I must remember what I need in order to be His vessel so His love may flow freely through me. I need to be empty of me, filled with Him. He is faithful to remind me He is in the cleaning up business. Once I surrender "my throne," He is free to cleanse me from the sinful prejudices that clog up my arteries. His Spirit is free to flow through me again. Do you know what that is like? Let me tell you. It is freedom! It is REAL life! It is GOD living through me! It is one of my very favorite things in all of life. God is helping me see others as He sees them. I have a new love for people I disdained before – I have HIS love. His love flows through me and they respond to HIM living in me. I can see it in their eyes. They know they are loved and respected as a person. They have no need to put up walls to defend themselves, nor is there a need to lash back at an offender. Their guard is let down and God's love can flow. What a privilege to be His vessel. All you have to do is ask. After all, it is HIS throne! Reign, Lord Jesus, reign!

I am writing to you as if you are a believer already. If you are not, I am hoping you will see all that you are missing and seek out your Father in Heaven. More than likely, God has placed at least one of HIS strange "creatures" around you. Hopefully they are living as the "salt of the earth" to enhance life, making Christianity attractive. Prayerfully, as His "light" to the world, we Christians are pointing to Jesus with our very lives. Ask one of these Christians to tell you more about their Jesus. Feel free to email me at susie.oberski@gmail.com – I would be honored to share more about my Lord!

What boggles my mind is those of you who have been introduced to Jesus and have tasted of His goodness; have heard Him speak but do not listen, have seen Him work in your life but have turned your eyes to earthly beauties – turn back to Him. Look into His face. He is calling. He is waiting.

God has powerfully used Christian songs in my life to help me see Him more clearly. I encourage you to limit other music in your life and allow God to fill you with Christian music, specifically worship. Even Christian music can have a lot of "feeling stuff" attached to it that centers more around you than focusing on God. Choose wisely what you allow into your heart, mind, and soul. Some of my favorite music comes through Integrity's Hosanna Music and Hillsong/Hillsong United. MUCH of their music incorporates scripture into their songs and I believe God's Spirit within us is fed and we grow. It also helps me memorize scripture when it is put to music. I was hoping to share the words of some of my favorite music with you throughout this book. Due to stiff copyright laws, I will be sharing only the name of the song and artist with a brief explanation of how each song ministered to me. Maybe you could care less – that is okay. If any strike a chord within you, please pursue further the songs God intends to feed your soul. **"Fill Me Up" by Don Poythress and Jared Anderson,**

Integrity 2009, is a song that I play over and over before I begin writing to remind me Who is writing this book and what HE wants us to HEAR and SEE through the words. It reminds me of my constant need for cleansing, surrendering my all, so that God can fill me with HIS ALL. May God use this book and the songs included to touch your heart and help you SEE as He would have you see – that **YOU are His MUCH MORE!**

CHAPTER 6

EARS TO HEAR

*"Jesus said, He who has ears to hear, let him hear…
…If anyone has ears to hear, let him hear."*
Mark 4:9, 23

Have you ever had someone just sit and listen to you adoringly? Have you ever taken time to just listen to someone? To listen to God? I cannot help but think God gave us two ears and one mouth for a reason…hmmm…maybe I am to listen more…MUCH MORE!

My Grandma Johnson was my adoring listener. We lived a couple of miles away from my Mom's parents and biked back roads over there during many of our summer days. Of course that was also the place to get lemonade, cookies, and ice cream any time we wanted. Hot tea with tons of milk and sugar in it (we didn't really like tea) and freshly baked banana bread was a regular treat after church on Sundays while we watched a Shirley Temple movie. We would lie in front of the television or snuggle by Grandma on the couch. Grandpa would be in his rocking chair and watch it with us but we knew we had to stay out of the way of him and his spittoon.

My favorite times were just sitting next to Grandma and listening to her many stories of growing up; she was a good storyteller. But the best of the best was when she would ask me questions about school, my bike rides, and playing out-doors (Scott was always Popeye, I was Olive Oil, and our neighbor/adopted brother, Bobby Grant, was Brutus). I could go on forever. She would intently listen to every word and smile her precious "Everything is okay" smile and hold my hand…I loved that! I knew when I was talking with Grandma, I was her very favorite in all of the world. Of course, we all thought we were her favorites but it was not disclosed until much later in life that she had no favorites. (I still think I was her favorite.)

One of the many great things about my Dad is that he would always make time for us. Owning your own business seems like a dream come true, but with it comes responsibility that does not end when you walk out of the door at the end of the day. Despite his "busy"ness, he always told us we could call him anytime of the day. He also would tell his employees if we called, no matter what he was doing, to put us through to him. One time I remember calling my Dad to tell him about falling and scraping my knee. At this time, we owned Hudson's Hardware and my Aunt Nell, Dad's sister, was working for him. Sure enough, Aunt Nell told me she would go get Dad for me. What I didn't know is that he was down in the basement way at the back of the store and I waited for 15 minutes for him to come and get my phone call. But he came. He listened. He reassured me I would live and that he loved me…and that he needed to get back to work to pay for that bandage! But he stopped what he was doing to listen to me…to turn his heart and ears to me.

It is a true gift to have someone really listen to you. Early on in my walk with Jesus, I knew I could always call on Him in prayer. I was taught much about prayer but I confess for the first half of my life my prayers were more about me and my wants. Then as I grew in my walk with the Lord, my prayers became more of an intercessory prayer, praying for others. I am slowly growing in an understanding that as MUCH as God wants me looking to Him, talking to Him, SO MUCH MORE He wants me to listen to Him. He wants a relationship with me, communicating back and forth WITH each other. THAT is one of the major differences between Christianity and any other religion. RELATIONSHIP. Jesus came for a relation-ship WITH us, to give us MUCH MORE than just a religion. The very best way to intercede for others is to ask God, their Creator, what they truly need. Sure, we can add the earthly essentials like, food, clothing, housing, good health and jobs. But none of this is going to make it through death. How about the eternal essential? A relationship with Jesus! For everyone to come to see, meet and KNOW the God of the universe, Who IS their deepest need. We may have no clue how that is going to come about but the exciting part is that God wants us to be a part of bringing everyone He brings into our life closer to being His…simply by LISTENING to Him in how He would have us pray…and then do it!

After we talk to God about someone, He may direct us to talk further with that person. Do we know our parents' greatest joy? Our siblings' worst fear? Our children's most priceless dream? Our spouse's deepest need? How well do we know our neighbor, employer, employee, doctor, mail person, gro-cery store clerk, school librarian, church janitor, our closest friend, and our most dreaded enemy? Why do you think they are in your life? Guaranteed, it is about relationship. If God cared enough about us to send Jesus so that we could have a relationship, might He have the very same purpose for the people in your life? There is ONE purpose for people in our lives. RELATIONSHIP! And if you are a Christian, your pur-pose is to introduce them to Jesus. However, no one wants to be a "project." We each need to know we are important whether we ever achieve anything or not. Jesus loves us PERIOD. We must allow Him to love others through us.

It is true that no one cares how much you know until they know how much you care. Learn the differences between what makes men and women tick. Learn the different spiritual gifts God gives Christians and come to appreciate a person for who they are. Find a good personality test to see how you and those in your life deal with life; what causes them to react and why they respond as they do. God is so wonderfully creative He has chosen to make us each unique. DO NOT expect everyone to be just like you. Learn to marvel at the differences. To have everyone the same would not be the adventure God intends us to have, nor could we accomplish the work God desires for us as a family or Church.

Ask God to show you different tools He has out in our world to help us understand people better. When my husband and I were newly married we were in a discipleship group; Michael with five other men, I was with five other women. We took a "test" on our spiritual gifts and learned out more about ourselves and each other. It has been HUGE in our life and marriage to shed light on understanding each other and other Christians, to see where they are coming from and why. We have gone to different marriage seminars, read Christian books, and sought out wise counsel, taking advantage of those "tools" God has placed in our lives. He wants to speak to us in so many ways. Our job is to listen so we can HEAR Him.

A few years ago we went to the seminar, Love and Respect, with Emerson and Sarah Eggerich. We always try to ask God to show us what He would have us hear and learn through every sermon, seminar, book, person, job, and life experience that He brings our way. We left the Love and Respect seminar in awe. Nothing new, in fact very basic. Truth straight from God's Word. The basic principle comes from Ephesians 5:33, husbands are "to love your wife as he loves himself, and the wife must respect her husband." Carry this understanding of a basic need into the lives of every male and female you know and you will come to grow in your relationship with each one. We ALL need love and respect but every woman thrives on love and every man thrives on respect. We also are all too familiar with the Crazy Cycle, as Emerson calls it: if the wife does not get love she does not give respect and if the husband does not get respect he does not give love. Around and around it goes. That is why it is called the Crazy Cycle; anytime we do the same thing over and over again with the same outcome that does NOT work is CRAZY!!! It is amazing when we look to God and follow His principles how much clearer our understanding and appreciation of others grows AND improves our relationships.

Most recently we read <u>Men Are Like Waffles, Women Are Like Spaghetti (Understanding and Delighting in Your Differences)</u> by Bill and Pam Farrel. Again, nothing new, BUT it hit home. It showed how women are like spaghetti; interwoven with EVERY thinking (and non-thinking) fiber within us, using every breathing moment of every day to interact with every person they know…and even those they do not know! Whew! Was that a bit rambling? See why it is exhausting being a woman!!! We are ALWAYS thinking about people!!! In other words, we are tuned in to relationships. In fact, women process life through relationships.

This confuses men because they are like waffles with everything compartmentalized. Each square is a holding place for each issue of life and one issue only. A "typical man lives in one box at a time and one box only. When a man is at work, he is at work. When he is watching TV, he is simply watching TV. That is why he looks as though he is in a trance and can ignore everything else going on around him. As a result, men are problem solvers by nature. They enter a box, size up the 'problem,' and formulate a solution" (pg. 11). Now this is where men and women get frustrated with each other (to put it mildly!) Most of the men's waffle squares are empty with NO WORDS. So if a woman asks a man a question and he is not "in" that square she thinks he is trying to hide something or doesn't care. A man cannot even fathom the need to have words if it isn't related to a specific job. It is not that he does not care. He simply sees no need for talking if it is not to fix something. Not wrong, different.

I cannot tell you how MANY times Michael has worked all day with a group of men and come home and knows nothing more about them than when he went that morning. However, the job gets done! Women on the other hand may not get a job done but they have comforted and cared for all the women involved...which energizes them to go home and finish the project (much more quickly if alone). Now I know to ask Michael if he is in a square with words or not before I ask him a question. He knows to ask me if I just want him to listen to my problem or to fix it. Not wrong, just different.

Please HEAR my heart, Ladies. After living with my Dad, brother, husband, and five sons, I think I have a pretty good idea about how men think and work. I truly believe most men are good, decent human beings who do not purpose to hurt or ignore you. Most will do anything if asked. Our problem as women is we cannot believe a living, breathing human being could be in a room and not SEE someone is hurting, or that something needs to be accomplished, i.e., taking the garbage out. Therefore, we will not ask. It does not get done unless we do it, which makes us angry. The man has no clue why you are upset, but figures you will tell him if you need something done...and another crazy cycle begins. It is up to us NOW to stop the cycle. Ask God to help you HEAR and understand the women and men in your lives. Ask Him to help you HEAR what makes their heart beat faster. How can you better encourage those in your life by fanning their flame? What a difference life will be when we come to appreciate the differences God has created among us!

My very favorite devotional is <u>My Utmost for His Highest</u> by Oswald Chambers, we call him "Ozzie." It was given to us years ago by our dear friend, Jane Naber, who at the time was a missionary in China. Ozzie says on May 22 that "God reveals in John 17 that His purpose is not just to answer our prayers, but that through prayer we might come to discern His mind." On February 13 he writes, "The goal of my spiritual life is such close identification with Jesus Christ that I will always hear God and know that God always hears me (see John 11:41)." What really grabs my heart is what he writes on February 7, "The purpose of prayer is that we get a hold of God, not of the answer."

How long have I been praying for the answer instead of seeing that Jesus IS the answer? How many times have I gone to the Celestial Vending Machine and put in my 60 minutes of prayer expecting to get my 60 requests answered? How many times have I gone to the throne to get answers instead of going to the throne to get Jesus, to just BE with Jesus?

It boggles my mind that God wants us to want Him as much as we want to be wanted by others...just for ourselves. Another devotional I read from the Sprangers (their story to follow) is <u>God Calling</u> by Two Listeners; edited by A. J. Russell. It is written as if God is speaking to these two listeners. On February 6 it says,

> "To the listening ear I speak, to the waiting heart I come. Sometimes, I may not speak. **I may ask you merely to wait in My Presence, to know that I am with you.** Think of the multitudes who thronged Me when I was on earth all eager for something. Eager to be healed, or taught, or fed.
>
> Think as I supplied their many wants, and granted their manifold requests, **what it meant to ME**, to find amid the crowd, **some one or two, who followed Me just to be near Me, just to dwell in My Presence.** How some longing of the Eternal Heart was satisfied thereby. **Comfort Me, a while, by letting Me know that you would seek Me just to dwell in My Presence, to be near Me, not even for teaching, not for material gain, not even for a message – but for Me. The longing of the human heart to be loved for itself is a something caught from the Great Divine Heart."**

Now to say that I would seek God to just dwell in His Presence without hearing a word from Him and being content in His Presence with silence is very different. Thankfully, we have His Word through the Bible with us but there are times I just want His nudge, His direction, to KNOW he hears me and is working. Sometimes He chooses silence and that is when I need to trust Him. Trust that He, through His Word, tells me,

IF I am obeying His Word, that He hears me and is working… in HIS time. Returning to the concept of faith goes where eyes cannot see and sometimes where ears cannot hear, reminds me to wait. How many times have I heard Him say, even in these silences or lack of action, "Susan, do you trust me or not? Either I am God all of the time or I am not God at all." **He IS my God of ALL**.

A great example of "presence" I have had is through the lives of my parent's lifelong friends, Bob and Zelda Grant. They are like second parents to us kids. We lived next door to them on Gallogly Road in Pontiac, Michigan and were over there every day during the summer to swim in their pool. We shared many a meal with them. When my parents bought a cabin up north, my Dad searched for the right one for Bob and Zelda to buy across the lake. In their retirement years, they both bought special places close to each other in Florida. We celebrated every 4th of July from early morning to late at night with them and their family, the Nybergs. We went hunting together, celebrated birthdays, graduations, weddings, babies, and held hands and hearts through too many funerals. Mom, Dad, and Bob have now all gone on to continue that friendship in Heaven and Zelda awaits that reunion. We await with her, continuing to hold hands and hearts – we are family, we are friends.

The example they taught us was to be present. I know that we have all heard that the greatest gift of all is your presence (maybe not appreciated quite so much when you are young – I, too, personally like presents ;). Of course, Bob and Zelda would not only bring gifts but would come at the beginning, help during, and leave at the end after everything was cleaned up. Whatever the occasion, they were there. Reliable. Consistent. Present. I did not even notice this lesson we were being taught until later in life when we started going to more and more funerals. Again, Bob and Zelda would come at the beginning of the visitation, love on us, and then often just sit quietly until the end. They wanted "just" to wait in our presence with NO expectation to be talked with, introduced, or thanked. They were there simply and ever so beautifully to support us. The next day Bob and Zelda would return for the funeral and do the same. They practiced this gift of being present in the lives of all those they knew, even the 1st, 2nd, and 3rd cousins! We used to joke about how Bob was related to everyone. The Grants had ears to hear the heart of the matter and be present.

How many times have I gone to visit someone and blown in and out like a tornado? How many times have I gone to a visitation just to make an appearance? How many times have I gone to the hospital to offer support and that thirty second prayer? How about you? I do not think my intentions, nor yours, were necessarily wrong, but how could I "do it" better? How MUCH MORE could God love through me if I practice being present for others? Just like everything else, the more you practice something, the more natural it becomes...just like breathing. Years ago I decided I wanted to have ears to hear any and all of God's promptings for me. I told Him I did not want to miss anything. I asked Him to do whatever it takes to get my attention and to help me be faithful to Him...to have ears to hear HIM!

God took me seriously! In June of 1999, Michael and I were going up to Sparrow Hospital to visit a family from our church who had just had their third child. We had stopped to turn right at the light on Pennsylvania and Michigan. Just as we started to turn, I noticed two runners sprinting across and pointed them out to Michael so that he would not hit them - never the best thing to do if you want to make a good first impression, unless with your tires! As they crossed in front of us, I felt a nudge...not even sure what it was or why I needed to "Notice those people." We parked our car and went into the hospital. As we got onto the elevator to go up to the 4th floor, "our" runners got on. I made silly small talk and as we got off at our floor, the woman reached out and said, "Please pray for our son." We said we would pray. The door closed. We prayed right then for God to be with those people and their son. Michael and I went on to see our friends and celebrate their newest of angels. When we left them we both looked at each other and agreed we needed to try to find "the runners" to see how we might be able to encourage them. We went up to the children's floor and looked in each room as we went by. No runners. One of the nurses had noticed us and asked if she might help us. We described our new "friends" and told them they had asked us to pray for their son. Right away she knew they were "The Sprangers" and had just gone down to the cafeteria. Crazily, we decided to pursue. Not sure what we were doing but feeling driven to connect, we went down to the cafeteria and wandered around, looking for the Sprangers. After our second time around, we thought we recognized them and went up and introduced ourselves. We told them we did not know why we were there but that we felt God had told us to seek them out. We found out they were from the Upper Peninsula, eight hours away, and they knew no one in Lansing. Their three year old son, Tucker, had been miraculously diagnosed with Neuroblastoma the day before by a small town doctor in Marquette. I say miraculously because he had a very rare disease that most doctors misdiagnose. They had sent them down to Lansing for the care of the specialists at Sparrow Hospital. The grandparents were there to support them but were leaving the next day. Michael said, "You can stay with us." I looked at him like he was crazy!!! With a tip of my head, raised eyebrows and THE stare, I half smiled and nodded in agreement. We prayed with them and exchanged our phone numbers so they could call us the next day to get to our house, fifteen minutes away.

We were quiet walking to the elevator. Once we were alone on the elevator, I asked, "What are we doing!!? We don't even know these people!" Michael said he just knew we had a house and we needed to offer it to the Sprangers. I agreed, but with hesitancy. Back home we had two boys off to college and three still living at home with three bedrooms upstairs and a fourth we had made in the basement. We had a 1 ½ bathrooms that we were used to sharing. But what about company?!!! How long would they stay? How would they be with our boys? What would they expect of us? Quietly, so quietly, I heard God say to me, "Susan, do you trust Me?" I answered, "Yes, Lord, but this is not quite what I had in mind when I told you I wanted to have ears to hear... nor did I have any idea this is how You planned to get my attention so I would not miss anything you needed me to do." Again, "Susan, do you trust Me?" We got home and told the boys about our adventure. We told them we had offered our house to STRANGERS! They thought it was great and could not wait to meet our new "friends." I was not quite so excited. I knew Michael would escape everyday to work and I would be the one to "entertain." Miss Hospitality I was not. I needed to be, I even sort of, kind of, wanted to be. I was more into having our boys' friends and youth group over. They were "safe," they were known. I was still in control. I could send them home when I was ready for "my" space. None of this am I necessarily proud of but I am letting you know my thought process during all of this; God's process for growing me to trust Him, to listen to Him, to be His. Selfishness I had to die to so that He could live through me.

Todd Spranger called the next day as planned and they came out for dinner that night. Kim and Todd were thin, tall gorgeous blondes in their early thirties and they brought Lauren, their adorable five year old daughter. Upon Tucker's diagnosis, Kim and Todd had notified their work to let them know of their need for an indefinite leave of absence. They had decided whatever happened, they needed to be together as a family. After dinner, Kim returned to the hospital and Todd and Lauren made their way to the basement bedroom. Kim and Todd took turns spending the night at the hospital with Tucker. Every morning, whichever parent was present, would join us with Lauren for breakfast before going up to the hospital to join Tucker. They did surgery to remove the tumor, followed by chemo and radiation. I don't even remember how long they were with us, most of the summer. They would go home for a short period of time and return for the next round of testing and chemo. Eventually Tucker had a bone marrow transplant. Lauren began Kindergarten in the fall in Marquette and the school worked with the Sprangers in her absence. Throughout this horrible trial, we saw Jesus lived out day and night through Todd, Kim, Lauren, and Tucker. They had energy and love galore for each other and for all those they encountered. They became a part of our family, part of our church family, a part of our neighborhood. Only one day do I ever remember seeing them struggle. Oh, they could have/ should have struggled everyday…but they did not. It was the day Tucker was having the bone marrow transplant and they knew the high risk to his little body. They CHOSE to trust God through this life experience, to listen to Him everyday, and to share each moment to bring glory to Him. Kim and Todd looked daily to God and saw Him living in their lives through His Word. In fact, Kim wrote a book about this experience, Riding God's Rainbow. God healed Tucker and the Sprangers are back in the Upper Peninsula. Today, Tucker and Lauren both are State champions in track and Todd is now in full time ministry. God surprised Kim and Todd last year, now in their early forties, with their third child, Will. Of course, they count this "surprise" as one of their greatest blessings! God blessed us with angels in our midst, all because we were willing to let Him get our attention.

In My Utmost for His Highest, on January 30, Ozzie calls this willingness to listen and obey God "the dilemma of obedience." He goes on to say, "God never speaks to us in dramatic ways, but in ways that are easy to misunderstand. Then we say, 'I wonder if that is God's voice?' Without the sovereign hand of God Himself, nothing touches our lives. Do we discern His hand at work, or do we see things as mere occurrences? Get into the habit of saying, 'Speak, Lord' (1 Samuel 3:9), and life will become a romance…as we listen, our ears become more sensitive, and like Jesus, we will hear God all the time."

I want to hear Jesus…I want so **MUCH MORE!!!**

CHAPTER 7

BEHOLD, THE LAMB

*"And the Word was made flesh, and dwelt among us,
and we beheld His glory, the glory of the One and Only
full of grace and truth…(when John first saw Jesus
coming to him he said,)
BEHOLD THE LAMB of God, Who takes away
the sin of the world
(and again after Jesus' baptism, John announces)
BEHOLD THE LAMB OF GOD."*
John 1: 14, 29, 36

Amidst a very cluttered, busy world, I struggle not to get distracted. Distracted from God. I never want Him to be trying to get my attention and not "get me." So back to being simple, I put on blinders. "Blinders?" you say, "typical Christian escaping reality!" No silly, not blinders to escape reality but to stay focused on God while I deal with reality. I do not want reality to distract me from God.

Raising five sons and being in the ministry can pull you in seventy jillion different directions. I am NOT saying we were any busier than any of you; we each have demands upon us that we need to sort out. Most demands we can and should let go of easily. For some reason, our society has told us the busier we are the more important we are. FALSE. We are just busier.

It does seem that everyone, including myself, is always more than happy to tell us what we should be doing. In fact, Michael has accused me several times of attempting to be the Holy Spirit in people's lives. Usually that happens when I am trying to get him to do something! Not to be blasphemous in the least, but I responded back that I would be the first to sign up if that "job" was ever offered. I would LOVE to be "hired" to tell people what to do, where to go, a nudge here, a push there, and convict them with TRUTH! Have I warned you? I am not a mercy.

When others are trying to "arrange" our lives for us, we need blinders to help us "Fix our eyes on Jesus, the Author and Perfecter of our faith." (Hebrews 12:2) In the verse before this, God tells us to "Throw off everything that hinders…and let us run with perseverance the race marked out for us." The point is that GOD marks the race for us, not anyone else! We may have very well meaning parents, friends, siblings, fellow parents and church members who think THEY are the ones to mark out our race. Now please know that if you are still under the authority of your parents, they do have the right and responsibility to help mark out your "race." I am all for submitting to God-given authority! This is when we need blinders to help us BEHOLD THE LAMB, looking for Jesus' smile alone. If He is smiling, it does not matter if anyone else is or not. If He is not smiling, do NOT do "it!!!"

You all know what I am talking about. There is no end to the list of good things we could be doing. People line up to get us on their committee, to sign us up for PTA, for helping at the concession stand for our kids' sporting events, to teach Sunday School, to be a Room Mom/Dad, to host a neighborhood picnic, or sing in the choir. For every person there seems to be a committee. None of these is bad, but the enemy of God's best is an endless list of good things. We only have so much time and energy. God wants to order our time so that we are freed to do His best.

A good way NOT to be asked again is to do something poorly, NOT on purpose, just not "gifted." **Once** our choir director invited everyone who loved to sing to come for the Easter Cantata practice. So I did! They handed me music and expected me to sing alto even though I was MUCH better hitting the notes I could find. Most notes hide from me. I was miserable! I suspect those around me were too. I did not smile all evening and I think singing is supposed to be fun! So the next morning, I went to tell our director (my favorite, Verona Nyquist!) I was going to step down. She simply said, "Ok", and turned with a sigh of relief! That was the last time I said YES to singing in the choir!

The word "No" is not the most popular answer. It is very freeing to enable you to say "yes" to whatever God needs you to do. Maybe it is simply staying home with your family, making cookies with your children. You do not need to explain your reason to say no. We are first accountable to God. If you are looking to Him, you need to allow Him to order your day to follow Him. Too many times I have overbooked my day and dreaded "the day the Lord hath made." How sad to ever dread His day! So when I come to my senses and cry out to Him to help me, I usually have phone calls come in to cancel out the crowded day. Talk about a personal God! Clearing my path! Sometimes I have to live with the consequences of <u>my</u> foolish scheduling. It is so much easier to start out at the beginning of each day with God marking out my race.

Michael is a very wise man. I feel very loved and protected by his leading of our family. One of the first things he would tell a ministry or church interviewing him is that they were not also hiring his wife. He also was up front in letting them know that his first priority was God, second was his wife, third was his children, so at best they were fourth. I know that has taken many a church member aback to think they were not first. However, when (if) they would think it through, they soon realized that if Michael was seeking God first that God would make sure they were also taken care of if there was a need.

No better way for me to start off my day than to **Behold The Lamb**...to fix my eyes on Jesus! This reminds me Who is, and who is not, in charge, which is so freeing and brings great peace. Sometimes I am feeling sad for various reasons. As I look to God, I hear Him say to me, "Susan, why are you downcast, why so disturbed? Put your hope in Me" (Psalms 42:5 personalized). Looking to Him enables you to see the SON, to see more clearly. Why enter any day before going to THE ONE Who has created it...THE ONE Who knows best for you? I have heard it said that it is best to tune up the instruments BEFORE the concert than afterwards.

"Constant Companion" by Bob Fitts, Integrity, reminds me to seek God at the beginning of my day, throughout the day, to listen for Him speaking to me. He will not compete with the noise of the world. We need to turn that off so we can hear His whispers. God offers us His all. God wants our all. Why do we try to do things on our own, looking to please people? **BEHOLD THE LAMB. He is SO MUCH MORE!!!**

CHAPTER 8

VINE LIFE

"I am the Vine; you are the branches.
If a man remains in Me and I in him, he will
bear much fruit; apart from Me you can do nothing."
John 15: 5

Warm, windy days are some of my favorite days. I love to walk outdoors and have the wind upon my face, dancing through my hair. To watch the trees bend almost in rhythm, swaying back and forth, leaves bouncing up, down, and all around while others fly through the air. How do some survive the winds and others break off in escape?

Do you ever watch people going through storms in their lives and wonder why some are able to stay calm, almost as if they are dancing in rhythm to the changing tides? They get on and off each wave of emotion with a confidence that they know what is at the end. Others ride the same waves and start sinking, flailing in a panic of fear. In horror they refuse to plunge into the water, thinking somehow that will rid them of dealing with the ride…as if closing off their emotions changes the outcome.

You watch people going through prime-time points in their lives. There are those who anticipate each moment breathlessly with joy and thankfulness. Then there are those who act as if life owes them something and they are finally getting their "due" reward.

I understand both extremes. Of course I do not want the bad times and always desire the good times. hat boggles my mind are those who shine through the days of drudgery...the daily routine with the same old beginning and the same old ending with all the sameness in the middle. Ozzie says on June 15 of <u>Utmost for His Highest,</u>

> "No one is born either naturally or supernaturally with character; it must be developed. Nor are we born with habits – we have to form Godly habits on the basis of the new life God has placed within us. We are not meant to be seen as God's perfect, bright-shining examples, but to be seen as the everyday essence of ordinary life exhibiting the miracle of His grace. Drudgery is the test of genuine character... Learn to live in those common times of the drudgery of life by the power of God. Earlier on March 6 he emphasized, "Live looking to God...ask God to keep the eyes of your spirit open to the risen Christ, and it will be impossible for drudgery to discourage you...never allow yourself to think that some tasks are beneath your dignity or too insignificant for you to do."

Vine life. What??? You say...vine life? No, VINE life. I am convinced that the reason you see healthy trees and plant life thriving through sunshine, storms, and drought is because their branches are connected to the vine, their source of life. In the same way, some people you see not only exist, but flourish through the ups, downs AND sameness of life. These are the ones connected to the Vine...to Jesus. John 15:4 says, "Abide in Me, and I will abide in you." To abide means to dwell, live with, breathing in and out. In many ways, it is making a habit out of being together. I like that. I like the idea of making a habit out of being with Jesus and Him being with me.

Do you know what it takes to build a habit? Three weeks. Behavioral scientists say it takes 21 consecutive days to build or destroy a habit. Ever go on a diet? Start eating healthy? Stop eating bad stuff? Start exercising? Stop smoking? Start reading your Bible daily? If you have, you will know it becomes natural, a habit, after three weeks. Now that does not mean it is necessarily easy. You still have to consciously choose your new lifestyle, breathing it in and out every day or you will revert back to your old "lifestyle."

I wanted God to be both Savior and Lord of my life. Although I was raised in a Christian home, accepted Jesus as my Savior at five years old, was baptized at eleven, and knew the value of reading my Bible, I had never made daily reading His Word a habit. I would read it one day and then skip a couple of weeks, read it for a couple of days and then skip three or four days. When I was a sophomore in college I decided that I wanted to be more than a church-going Christian. I wanted to have Jesus living with me, abiding day in and day out. I also knew it was God's will for me to be in His Word and with Him daily.

I believed John 14:14, "You may ask Me for anything in My Name, and I will do it." I asked God to help me read a minimum of one chapter a day for the rest of my life. I also asked Him to not let me go to sleep if I had not read His Word that day. That was 36 years ago and He has not failed to take me at my word because I took Him at His Word. My goal is not one chapter a day but to be with Him in His Word. Upon rare occasion, I have grabbed a quick Psalm to "get in" my one chapter. I can count on one hand the times I have gone to bed and laid there awake. I usually hit my pillow and am asleep and then His Spirit touches my shoulder and reminds me of my vow to Him to be in His Word daily...so I get up and read. How cool is that?!!! Our God is a God Who is intimately involved in our lives and wants us to fulfill our promises, wants us to know Him.

God not only wants us to know Him, He wants us to have a life of complete joy. Not necessarily happiness, or an easy, carefree life, but one filled with His JOY. **HE completes us**. Jesus tells us in John 15:9–11, "As the Father has loved Me, so have I loved you. Now remain in My love. If you obey My commands, you will remain in My love, just as I have obeyed My Father's commands and remain in His love. I have told you this SO THAT My JOY may be in you and that your JOY may be COMPLETE." How can we not have joy if we feel complete? Better yet, KNOW we are complete because JESUS says so! Some of my most difficult times have been when I felt an emptiness, as if something or someone is missing. Again, God calls me back to His Word and asks me if I trust Him. I choose to believe I am complete BECAUSE He says so. So many times I want to wrap myself up in feelings…God tells me to wrap myself up in Him.

I have had people ask me how it is so easy for me to eat right, exercise daily, be in His Word daily, and be thankful. They say I must have a strong will power. I reply it is more like a God empowered "won't power." To become disciplined means I choose to train towards an expected end of moral/mental improvement, specifically one that will assist my MASTER in spreading His teachings. The root word of discipline is disciple, a person who subscribes to the teachings of a master and assists in spreading them.

My three favorite things in all of the world after Jesus and my family, is SLEEP, ICE CREAM, and hot FRENCH FRIES! I am NOT a morning person nor a night person…in fact, my prime time is 10 a.m.–2 p.m. Catch me before or after that and all I can say is "Good luck!" Our boys learned early that if they needed help with homework it was pretty much useless after 9:00 p.m. Ok, it was useless before that too, but they did not learn that until they were about ??? 13 when the "higher math" kicked in. Thankfully they had a smart Daddy and as the boys got older I would just point the younger ones to an older one… one reason we kept having children – for their brains and their "free" labor!

Years ago God spoke to me and reminded me I had asked Him to be Lord of my life, to allow Him to be my Master. He pointed me to I Corinthians 6:12, "Everything is permissible for me but not everything is beneficial. Everything is permissible for me, but I will NOT be mastered by anything." I think this came after one of my binges with my sister, Kaye, when we would decide to go on a diet. That evening, up until midnight, we would eat all we could, specifically piles and piles of ice cream with caramel, fudge and pecans on top, Of course we would be so sick the next day we would not want to eat anything so cutting calories for awhile was not difficult. We came to realize we had to choose a healthy eating lifestyle, not just a diet until we lost the weight we wanted and then go back to our old eating habits.

The same with sleeping…I asked God to help me get the sleep my body needed, not wanted, and trust Him to energize me throughout the day for whatever HE needed. "Apart from Me you can do nothing" (John 15:5). That included exercising. Yes, that meant I would get less sleep in order to fit it in my schedule but exercising actually gives me more energy for the day; MUCH MORE energy to be used of God. My favorite exercise is walking. It used to be jogging but walking is MUCH better because I can actually breathe! Another HUGE benefit God pointed out to me in exercise was it gave me marvelous time with Him alone. Nothing puts me in a more worshipful state of mind than being out in His creation. It takes me off of my throne and puts Him on His rightful throne – so I can rest in whatever follows in the day because I know God is in charge.

Those who know me are quite aware I am fffaaaarrrrr from perfect. For those whom I have never met, please hear my heart. When I was a young Mom, there was many a day I was exhausted because life with little ones was often 24/7. Yet I wanted to still meet with God daily, to read His Word, to listen to His Words of love for me and to share my heart with Him. The day would often blend into day with the only difference being it was dark during the "night" day. I would still get up, often with a child in arms, to meet with God. I would fall asleep. Satan would make so much fun of me and make me feel (there is that "feel" word again) so guilty. He would mock me and call me "Super Christian." He would laugh and say what a hypocrite I was to try to have any semblance of a quiet time with my "so called" God and then falling asleep…"Some Christian YOU are!"

~~~ A side note: Satan is the accuser, you know? Anytime you are clear before God and start "feeling" guilty or discouraged or depressed, it is NOT God. God may convict, but His convictions specifically direct us to life, a change for His best and our best. God breathes in life to us so as to encourage, lift up and fan His flame within us. Always make sure you are listening to the right voice. A wise friend once told me it doesn't matter whose voice you hear AS LONG AS GOD RECEIVES THE GLORY. Satan will stop bothering you if every time he whispers in your ear you turn it around to point to Jesus for HIS praise and HIS glory! He stopped waking me at night years ago because I would start praying. ~~~

Back to falling asleep during quiet time with little ones still home…GOD reminded me ever so gently that He was quite aware that He had given me these precious children and He even knew their schedules, and my lack of sleep. He ever so lovingly looked in my eyes and said how MUCH He loved that I would STILL get up to meet with Him and it was more than enough if I just wanted to climb up on His lap and listen to His heart beat. He would hold me and refresh me…sometimes while feeding a child or many a time in the middle of the night calming both me and our child. Remember, He is a pro at calming the storms!

An all time favorite daily prayer I have personalized for our family is Colossians 2:6, 7 & 10, "Just as we have received You, so may we walk (and talk) with You, (being lovers of and leaders for You) being rooted, built up, established in the faith and abounding with thanksgiving…**knowing** we are **COMPLETE** in You." We must be rooted, connected to the Vine, our very Source of life. How else do we intend to live in this life with joy? We are **COMPLETE IN CHRIST**, not dependent on anyone or anything else to complete us. We are free to look to Him, wait on Him, be filled by Him.

To be filled by Christ, we must be emptied of ourselves. In 1986, my Dad ended up back in the hospital for open heart surgery. It was awful. To say it was one of those roller coaster experiences is an understatement. Again, my Mom was a rock, because she was trusting God and anchored in Him, her Rock. I was trying to, but I could not imagine life without my Dad. Four of our five boys had been born by this time. I wanted them to know their Grandpa and be able to have many more years with him, and he with them. After surgery we were able to sneak back for a few moments to see Dad. It was the first time I had seen someone on a respirator. He was all bloated after the surgery and was being kept alive by a machine. I have never felt so panicky, so useless to help my Dad. I still get teary eyed just thinking about it. I rushed out of the room and Kaye tried to calm me, but I did not want to be calmed. I scurried blindly down a hall to be by myself. I needed space. I needed time to process all of this. I wanted to bury my head in Michael's arms and cry but he had wonderfully freed me to be up at the hospital with my family while he stayed home with the boys. I found an empty waiting room with a window facing the hospital's helicopter landing pad. As I looked out, my eyes were drawn to a flag flapping in the wind. It kept changing directions. Then I heard God say to me, "Susan, you are like that flag, letting your emotions guide you like the wind guides the flag. I want you to allow Me to be your Guide. I want you to empty yourself of all you are so that I can fill you with all of Me. Let me complete you. Let go of all of your hopes and expectations that you have in life…in Michael, your boys, health for your Dad, friendships, growth in your ministry and let Me be your Hope and Expectation. Let Me fill you, let Me complete you."

I thought back to John 15 where God tells us He is the Vine, we are the branches…without Him, we can do nothing. Like my Dad's bad arteries and veins that needed cleaning out and replacing, I needed to allow God to empty me of me, cleanse me, and fill me with Him. Do you know we have the power to stop God? He will NOT force His ways or His will on us. I was stopping God by holding onto my ways. Right then I asked God to cleanse me of all that I am and fill me with all that He is…to fill me with His Spirit. I asked Him to keep me sensitive to His Spirit, to immediately tap my shoulder or to do whatever it takes to get my attention if I started taking over. Never again did I want to hinder His Spirit from moving; leading my life in His direction, down the path of His choice. I wanted my "root system" to be in Him, for Him to be my nourishment, my Source of Vine Life!

When we are willing to die to ourselves and live unto Jesus, people notice. GOD gets the glory. I think of the apostles, Peter and John, in Acts 3 and 4 when they were getting themselves in trouble for believing Jesus and living out their faith. They had allowed God to heal the crippled man through them and were CONVINCED that "Salvation is found in no one else, for there is no other name under Heaven given to men by which we must be saved" (Acts 4:12). The Priests and Sadducees (sad, you see, because they did not believe in the resurrection) were puzzled how they were to keep Peter and John from teaching about Jesus. Acts 4:13 says, "When they saw the courage of Peter and John and realized that they were unschooled, ordinary men, they were astonished and they took note that THESE MEN HAD BEEN WITH JESUS."

Do people know that we have been with Jesus? Have we? Are we abiding with Him daily, dwelling with Him, breathing in and breathing out His Word? Are we convinced that salvation is found in no one else but JESUS? Are we able to say, like Peter and John in Acts 4:19, "Judge for yourselves whether it is right in God's sight to obey you rather than God. For we cannot help speaking about what we have seen and heard." What have we seen? What have we heard? God promises us if we choose to abide in Him, He abides in us. He will fill us. He will complete us. He will bear MUCH fruit through us…but we have to be connected to Him, the VINE.

Another all time favorite book of mine is <u>The Vine Life</u> by Colleen Townsend Evans. It is a very basic book about abiding with Jesus. On page 25 she mentions that "Grapevines have to have full sun to be healthy and bear good fruit. Shady places make them susceptible to mildew." Although this sounds pretty obvious, it was an excellent reminder to me that I needed to be exposed daily to Jesus, my Light. It also was clear that allowing any shade or darkness in my life was asking for trouble. It was potentially weakening and eventually killing off His Life Source in me, the branch.

We humans think we can do everything, even abide. <u>The Vine Life</u> on page 63 continues to say, "It is only the life of the Vine in the branch that makes the branch able to do anything – even to abide…abiding should contain no strain or effort; it is rest from effort. The natural branch certainly need not strain to remain a part of the vine; it simply is. All it needs to do is STAY CONNECTED" (page 72). My responsibility is to live a connected life, as the branch to the Vine. The responsibility for the fruit was God's, He is the Vinedresser's. We know from Galatians 5: 22-23, "The fruit of the Spirit is love, joy, peace, patience, kindness, goodness, faithfulness, gentleness and self-control." Through our fruit, people will know whether or not we have been with Jesus.

Happiness is conditional. It is dependent on external happenings in our lives. Joy, and all the rest of the fruit, are dependent "on a great act that has happened to us internally. The Bible does not say joy is a fruit of circumstances; it states that joy is a fruit of the Spirit. Joy is the evidence of God in our lives" (<u>Vine Life</u>, page 97). God tells us in Nehemiah 8:10 that "The joy of the Lord is your strength." The possessive OF THE LORD shows it is the LORD's JOY…His joy, my strength. That explains a lot to me on the days I FEEL joyless but He radiates through me with HIS JOY.

Everyone enjoys the beauty and aroma of a fresh flower arrangement. However, it is only days before the flowers start drooping and petals begin to fall off because they have been cut off from their vine. Flowers connected to their vine continue to grow, bud, and produce more flowers and a pleasing fragrance for all. As we abide in Christ, may we "Spread everywhere the fragrance of the knowledge of Him. For we are to God the aroma of Christ among those who are being saved and those who are perishing" (II Corinthians 2:14, 15). May God draw others to Himself because we have been with Jesus and are convinced He is the Source of all life.

May we be His MUCH MORE to those around us, for His praise and glory!

CHAPTER 9

SO THAT
I AM
NEVERTHELESS

*"I keep asking that the God of our Lord Jesus Christ,
the **glorious Father**, would give us the Spirit of
wisdom and understanding **SO THAT** we would **know
Him better**. I pray also that the **eyes of our heart
would be enlightened in order that we would know
the hope** to which He has called you, the riches
of **His glorious inheritance** in the saints, and **His
incomparably great power** for us who believe."*
Ephesians 1: 17 - 19

This was never intended to be one of the chapters. I had made a list of what I thought God wanted for chapter titles and thoughts but He took me seriously in this being HIS book...can you imagine?! What boldness! What authority! In fact, as I started to write the next chapter, I very much felt God say, "Uh uhh, not yet – I want, **So That I Am Nevertheless**." I even asked Him if He was sure. He was quite sure! I was the one not so sure. When I shared it with Michael, he looked at me and even kind of wrinkled his nose saying, "It does not easily flow." Flowing is way over rated when God wants something. So bear with me. God gets His way.

Actually, I get very excited when God interrupts my writing with HIS writing, HIS thoughts. I felt like God was saying to me that I needed to expound on abiding in His Word...that I needed to let you know that I am not always excited about reading His Word...'specially Leviticus, Numbers, I and II Chronicles and the R-rated Song of Solomon. I really love Genesis, Deuteronomy, Joshua, Ruth, I Samuel, the first three and last five chapters in Job, Isaiah, Daniel and Jonah. All of the New Testament is amazing and a joy to read, especially John, Romans, Colossians and Hebrews. Trying to soak it all in and live it is another thing. This is where He comes in... again ☺

For years I have read the Bible. I wanted to know all of it. Before I was married I was determined to read through the Bible every year. After we were married we were challenged to read through the Bible with a reading schedule. We would read on average three chapters a day in the Old Testament and two to three chapters a day in the New Testament in order to get through the OT once and the NT three times a year. That was wonderful but, for me, a very stringent schedule. If I lagged behind I would skim the chapters to catch up. Or, confession time, read just my underlined section because that really was MY IDEA of the best part. I would feel guilty for not "keeping up" with what I (not God) imposed on myself. I always finished the "schedule" and even tho' skimming at times, there was value in learning an overview of the Bible.

I believe God wants me to tell you I have also had many dry times in my Bible reading. There were times when I read just to read but was not getting anything out of it and questioned the value of my reading it. Please hear me, I question NOT the value of the Bible but the value of my time reading it. Is there value in the Bible if it is not read? Seriously. Did God have His Book written to just sit on our shelves? No, He wrote it to us **SO THAT** we would come to know the great **I AM is NEVERTHELESS**!

Just this morning we had an early morning phone call that shook the ground beneath us. Our youngest son, Matt, is a sophomore at the University of Michigan (Go Green!) and lives in a dorm with three other great guys. His best friend and roommate, Dave, called us around 7:30 a.m. to say that Matt had just had a seizure. Our hearts dropped. This had also been one of my greatest fears with him being two hours away at college. He was okay, but Dave had called the EMT's just to make sure. They came and decided the worst was over and he would just have to sleep it off. As Matt later said, they asked him a lot of "orientation" questions and he passed most of them! The great news was that Matt was okay. He had seized while still in bed, so had not fallen and hurt himself. This was not the first time.

This "adventure" started January 6, 2001, a little over nine years ago. I am not going into detail except to say he started with a grand mal seizure and has been on medication ever since. Thankfully, the type of seizures he has only happen as he is waking, but he does have grand mal seizures and they are terrifying. Again, thankfully, God has controlled them with medication and in this amount of time Matt has "only" had nine seizures, including the one this morning. After going two years without any seizures, doctors believe it is safe to try to wean a person off the medication. We did that once and only three days after being medicine free Matt had another seizure. This time it had been two years and three months since a similar seizure had occurred while he was awakening and still in bed. Without comparing notes, Matt had mentioned to friends his thoughts about maybe being able to go off of his meds. I had just last week prayed, thanking God for protecting Matt from seizures and wondering if he was healed, asking if there was a way we could know without risking his protection. ARGH! As awful as this morning was, God answered our questions. Very safely He let us know now is not the time. I get chills thinking about how personal the great I AM is, how intimate, how **He is NEVER THE LESS!** As Michael and I were sitting on the couch after "the call," we could do little but pray, our

70

focus on Matt. Outside our window flew a robin and just sat on the branch for the longest time. God always uses birds to remind me of His care. Again I heard, "Susan, do you trust Me? Remember, I love Matt even more than you do."

I had just read in Deuteronomy 33:26-27, "There is no one like the God of Jeshurun (a term of endearment meaning the beloved one), Who rides on the heavens to help you and on the clouds in His majesty. (Isn't that elegant?!!!) THE **ETERNAL GOD** is your refuge, and underneath are the **everlasting** arms." Yes, Lord, I remember, and I thank You for keeping Your everlasting arms underneath and around Matt, holding him close to Yourself. As difficult as this is, I even thank You for allowing the seizure **SO THAT** we would **REMEMBER You are NEVERTHELESS!**

So back to those dry times and schedules. **God wants us to want HIM. God wants us to seek HIS face, HIS smile**. God wants us to ask HIM what HE wants us to hear from HIS Word, to approach HIM boldly, with confidence of HIS love and HIS desire to be with us, to speak to us personally. God tells us in Hebrews 4:16, to "Approach the throne of grace with confidence, **SO THAT** we may receive mercy and find grace to help us in our time of need." He sings to us in Psalm 100:4, to "Enter His gates with thanksgiving and His courts with praise; give thanks to Him and praise His name." Do we feel like we are not getting past first base? Does the door remain closed? Are we approaching Him as He instructs us with thanksgiving **SO THAT** the gates are opened? Do we stand inside HIS courts praising HIM or giving Him our list of wants?

I know some (okay, maybe many) of you think I am a little (okay, maybe a lot) wacko when I say God speaks to me. But He does. I want to show you how God speaks to me by going back to one of my least favorite books, beginning with Leviticus. A few years ago I went boldly before the throne of God and told Him what He already knew; that I was not getting much out of Leviticus and needed help. I felt Him smile, pleased that I was finally taking Him seriously. So I turned to

Leviticus with new eyes, NOT to get through a schedule or to read every word but to hear what the great I AM had to say to me! The very first line said, "The Lord called to Moses and spoke to him." GOD SPOKE TO MOSES! If God would speak to Moses, I knew He wanted to speak to me! So, excitedly, I said, "Speak, Lord!" Throughout Leviticus I saw things I had never seen before!

What was huge for me is how over and over again it says that "The Lord said to Moses…" I also am so touched by how God spoke to me about the many offerings He talks about in Leviticus, that they are to be PLEASING TO THE LORD. The light came on! My life is to be my offering, lived in such a way that it is PLEASING TO THE LORD. I needed to put blinders on and look for HIS smile alone. I was reminded that our offerings are to be brought BEFORE THE LORD, made TO THE LORD. **WE** are to be an aroma PLEASING TO THE LORD! Are we? Over and over it says that Moses did "As the Lord commanded." Do we obey all God commands? Why do we wonder when we are not blessed? Why do we question God and His answers when we choose to enter HIS GATES with our rules? In Leviticus 9:6, "This is what the Lord has commanded you to do, **SO THAT** the glory of the Lord may appear to you." Do you want to see Jesus? Obey Him. Do all He commands.

Continuing in Chapter 18 of Leviticus, God starts reminding us in a new way that "**I AM** the Lord your God." In 24:2, God tells us to "Bring clear oil … for the light SO THAT the lamps may be kept burning continually." We are the light of whom He is speaking! God wants us to be free of sin **SO THAT** His Spirit can flow through us for all those around us to see HIS Light continually! I love that!

Just as a parent lays down rules for their children, our Father God lays out rules for us, His children. In Chapter 26, He tells us about His rewards for obedience. In Chapter 27, He makes clear His punishment for disobedience. This is emphatically repeated in Deuteronomy 28. One of our most helpful statements to our boys as they were growing was shared with us by Todd and Connie Graham, who raised beautiful, God-adoring children. It was simply, "If you choose to disobey, you will be disciplined." Our job as parents was to clearly lay down the rules with the rewards for obedience and the punishment for disobedience. It was our sons' job to obey or not to obey with consequences following for their actions. So if they were spanked (and yes, we spanked), it was because THEY CHOSE to disobey the rules, not because we were mean. So rather than fighting with them all day long to be good, whenever they would have "that look" we would simply say, "If you choose to disobey, you will be disciplined"… and then follow through. After all, we were the parents, the adults, we were in charge. Why do we ever expect our children to obey us when we choose not to obey our Father in Heaven?

~~~ Side note: We are quite aware we are NOT perfect parents, nor do we have perfect children – I do think they are pretty close. We did not always do it right and God had to show us what each of our children needed in discipline, love and encouragement as they were each wonderfully unique. Again, in God's great wisdom, we had John first, our easiest to discipline. If we had had Danny first, he probably would have been an only child ☺ Michael and I had hoped that the rest would be easy like John. Nope. Goes to show God has a sense of humor! **James Dobson**, in his book, **The Strong Willed Child,** could have done his research through the O'Berski Family. **PLEASE hear that the principles we used from scripture are there to equip our children for life – each child still had the freedom to choose right from wrong**. Our faith is in God, not "perfect" parenting tools. We trust God with our children. God does not care as much if we are successful parents as He cares that we are faithful to Him and His ways.

So my "new" way of reading God's Word was becoming quite exciting, "New every morning" (Lamentations 3:23). The Lord continued to "talk" to me throughout Numbers. It boggled my mind that over and over again Numbers repeated "The Lord spoke to Moses." Then Moses spoke to God! He often cried out to God, making wise appeals on behalf of God's people, but more so on behalf of God's reputation. If God spoke to Moses, **SO MUCH MORE** He wants to speak to you and me! If Moses spoke to God, **SO MUCH MORE** He wants us in that same relationship, oneness, communing with the great **I AM**! Leviticus and Numbers came alive for me, showing me how orderly my God is and why. Why? **SO THAT** we would be ready to work (Numbers 8:11) and show the other nations the great **I AM is NEVER THE LESS!**

~~~ Another Side note: **Nevertheless** is one of my favorite words but it is not used in NIV…the words, **But God** often is… check out the passages below…see how they point to GOD and make the scripture come alive! It is alive!!!

***Hebrews 4:12 says, "For **the Word of God is LIVING** and active. Sharper than any double-edged sword, it penetrates even to dividing soul and spirit, joints and marrow; it judges the thoughts and attitudes of the heart."

***Acts 2:22–24, "Jesus of Nazareth was a man accredited by God to you by miracles, wonders and signs, which God did among you through Him, as you yourselves know. This man was handed over to you by God's set purpose and foreknowledge; and you, with the help of wicked men, put Him to death by nailing Him to the cross. **BUT GOD** raised Him from the dead, freeing Him from the agony of death, because it was impossible for death to keep its hold on Him."

***Galatians 2:20 (KJV), "I am crucified with Christ, **NEVERTHELESS** I live; yet not I, but Christ liveth in me: and the life that I now live in the flesh I live by the faith of the Son of God, Who loved me, and gave Himself for me."

Don Poythress and Tony Wood wrote a great song called "**Expectation,**" **(Integrity, 2009).** In it they beautifully explain how we need to come with open hearts to the Lord with expectation and celebration, anticipating what He holds in store for us. Expect to be changed by the power of His Word whenever we come before Him seeking His face in worship and with praise!

START. Ask God to show you what HE wants you to hear from HIM. Be ready, expectant, for Him to speak to you, for words to jump out at you like never before. Words like Sovereign, meaning to have supreme rank or power, stood out as **SOveREIGN** – So Reign, Lord…look up in your concordance and you will see it usually is spoken "**SOveREIGN LORD**"…So Reign, Lord! Isaiah 40:10-11 says, "See, the **Sovereign Lord** comes with power, and His arm rules for Him…He tends His flock like a shepherd: He gathers the lambs in His arms and carries them close to His heart; He gently leads those that have young." Does that not make you want to shout, **SO REIGN, LORD!!!**?

Ozzie in <u>Utmost for His Highest</u> says (March 18) that I have "the responsibility to keep my spirit in agreement with His Spirit." In <u>God Calling</u> (March 16), "Do you realize that I am telling you Truths, revealing them, not repeating oft-told facts. Meditate on all I say. Ponder it. NOT to draw your own conclusions, but to ABSORB MINE. All down the ages, men have been too eager to say what they thought about My Truth, and so doing, they have grievously erred. Hear Me. Talk to Me. Reflect Me. Do not say what you think about Me. My Words need none of man's explanation. I can explain to each heart."

God wants us to come to Him expectantly, boldly, with confidence **SO THAT** the great **I AM** can be **NEVERTHELESS** in each one of our lives through His living Word. Once we come face to face with the Great **I Am**, He never wants us to leave unchanged.

DO NOT SETTLE FOR ANYTHING LESS THAN HIS BEST! WE are HIS MUCH MORE!!!

CHAPTER 10

BECAUSE I SAID SO

*"Just as He who called you is holy, so be holy in all
you do; for it is written: Be holy, because I am holy."*
I Peter 1:16

Back to that parenting thing, we often think, if not say, "Obey me because I said so, I am the boss!" Years ago, while reading I Peter, I found that God says the same thing, "Because I said so (for it is written), be holy!" The difference? He really IS **THE** Boss! How often do we take His Word as just words instead of THE WORDS from the mouth of God, THE ONLY ONE with AUTHORITY?!! We often take others more seriously. As mentioned in the last chapter, God lays down the rules, it is our job to obey them. Of course we have a choice, but we also have the consequences; reward or punishment. As a child, we learn to obey to avoid the punishment. As we grow, we obey to receive the rewards. Continuing in our growth and relationship with our parents, our motivation to obey is because we desire to please them.

Except for the first eighteen months of my childhood, I was a fairly easy child to raise - if you do not count the last 55 years! At birth, my legs were turned in and so my parents agreed with the doctors to put me in casts, followed by braces, and finally funky shoes to correct them. It worked, and

I am thankful! I also had colic and was one ornery little girl. Besides that, I truly was fairly easy because I always wanted to please my parents...I adored them. I also knew they were usually right and I could trust them.

I believe that is how it is in every relationship. We grow in our understanding of people; those we can trust and those we cannot trust. Whether it be with parents, friends, teachers, employers, spouses, or children, we learn through the many seasons of life the people we can take at their word. We hear different inflections or see different looks and know when they are teasing or when they are serious. We come to know those who are right and those who are usually wrong. It is always easier to obey or follow through with something when we can trust someone. Much is based on our history with them.

My parents were excellent parents and I loved them dearly. They were consistent in their outpouring of love and firm discipline. No doubt, they were a team in parenting, and we all knew if one said "No" to something, we would be crazy to go to the other one and ask, hoping to get a "Yes." That would be double trouble! However, my Dad would sometimes say something I always thought was awful; "Do as I say, not as I do." That was something I did not want to emulate. So as a parent, I desired to model for our boys whatever I said was necessary and not give them mixed messages. I did fairly well except for always driving the speed limit...I did try not to go under...and eating all things...ok, what I like...and in moderation...except for ice cream!

God has quite a history! In fact, He created it! However, I recognize everything still goes back to relationship. If you know of God, you know He is to be revered and think He is probably someone you can trust. But once you come to KNOW God, you hold Him in reverence and know He is THE ONE you can trust. When He speaks, you want to listen. Where He leads, you want to follow. What He says, you want to obey, even when you do not like it or agree. Why? BECAUSE you can trust Him!

There are many who say you should never argue with God, never question God. For sure, to argue with God is foolish in the sense you will always lose...and God is always right so why question Him? BUT, I believe this always go back to relationship. When you know someone loves you and they know you love them, opening up your soul to one another is what grows that relationship. To disagree or question something is not wrong. I believe it helps you understand where the other one is coming from better. We see evidence of this in a few chosen dialogues from the Bible with God's soul mates', Abraham, Moses, Hannah, and Mary (just to name a few). Their very conversations with God showed their intimate relationship, their honor, and their trust in His wisdom. God knew their heart as well. He listened and adjusted His plans because of their appeals.

Abraham pleads for God to spare Sodom. In Genesis 18:23–32, Abraham appeals to God on behalf of the righteous who may remain. God knows Abraham is desirous of protecting His reputation, "Far be it from You to do such a thing – to kill the righteous with the wicked...will not the Judge of all the earth do right?" Abraham begins by asking to spare Sodom if 50 righteous people can be found, and each time God agrees he goes down lower to 45, then 40, 30, 20, and finally with continued boldness to 10. Such audacity! I would have been afraid God would strike ME dead! Relationship. God knew Abraham's heart and agreed. Sadly, there were not 10 righteous in Sodom and it and Gomorrah were destroyed.

Several times Moses approached God but my very favorite appeal is in Exodus 32. Moses had come down off of the mountain after being there for 40 days with God writing out the Ten Commandments. During this time, Aaron and the Israelites had made a golden calf. God, in His righteous anger, said in verse 7, "Go down because YOUR people, whom YOU brought out of Egypt, have become corrupt." God was ready to destroy them all. In verses 11–14, "Moses sought the favor of the Lord, His God...why should Your anger burn against YOUR people (nobody wanted them!) Whom You brought out of Egypt with great power and a mighty hand? Why should the Egyptians say it was with evil intent that He brought them out, to kill them in the mountains and to wipe them off the face of the earth? Turn from Your fierce anger; relent and do not bring disaster on YOUR people...then the Lord relented and did not bring on His people the disaster He had threatened." Wowser!!! GOD relented BECAUSE Moses questioned Him and appealed for His reputation and the life of His people! Boldness! Respect for one another! Relationship!

God uses His Word to reveal to us His desire for intimacy, wanting us to come before Him with our appeals. In 1 Samuel, chapter 1, Hannah desperately wanted a child and cried out to the Lord, sharing her heart's desire. She was not saying God was wrong, she was again and again requesting that He hear her heart and bless them with a child. In reverence, she pleaded. The next morning, Hannah and her husband, Elkanah, went and worshiped before the Lord. They were not angry with God. God was not angry with them. God honored Hannah's request.

Mary, the mother of Jesus, questioned God when she was told she was going to be a mother of the Son of God. She knew she was a virgin. She was not questioning God's wisdom, power, or authority. She was questioning how it was humanly possible. In Luke 1:34-38, Mary simply asks, "How will this be...since I am a virgin?" The angel reminded Mary, "Nothing is impossible with God." Mary quickly submitted to God's will, "I am the Lord's servant." God knew her heart. Is that not the heart He wants for each of us? Is that not the mission He purposes for each of us...to be God's servant, wherever, however, whenever?

There are so many things I do not understand in the Bible. Or maybe it seems quite clear in the Bible until it is "played" out in MY life. I go before God in reverence asking Him to help me understand. I am neither questioning Him nor His right to say or do anything He wants. I am asking for clarification. I want to know Him more. I want to learn His ways. If I do not understand, it is hard for me to follow. He knows my heart. I am

His and He is mine. We have a relationship. Many times God may answer or clarify my questions through other Scripture or sometimes through Godly teaching. His Light often comes on as I go through everyday life experiences and I think, "Ah hah! Now I get it!"

I must add here that there have been, are, and will be times I do not understand, He chooses not to clarify, and I still need to follow. Often I understand later, but not always... however, I do always come to know God more intimately. I am reminded He is ALWAYS good, just, kind, loving, wise, and ever faithful. God reminds me in I John 2: 3, "We know that we have come to know Him IF we obey His commands." What commands?!!! If we do not know what is going on and why, how can we obey? Something I have come to see and know very clearly is that we may not know why something is happening or what we can even do about it, BUT we ALWAYS know we are to love and pray. These are commands and principles we see over and over in the Bible. Jesus demonstrated countless examples of loving and praying throughout His life...in the good times and in the awful times.

A favorite Truth in the Bible for me is in II Kings 5 where Naaman meets Elisha. A little overview is that Naaman is a commander of the army of the king of Aram and he had leprosy. His wife's servant girl knew of God's power to heal and told Naaman's wife about God's prophet Elisha. In verses 9 –14, we see that,

> *"Naaman went with his horses and chariots and stopped at the door of Elisha's house. Elisha sent a messenger to say to him, 'Go, wash yourself seven times in the Jordan, and your flesh will be restored and you will be cleansed.' But Naaman went away angry and said, 'I thought that he would surely come out to me and stand and call on the name of the Lord his God, wave his hand over the spot and cure me of my leprosy. Are not Abana and Pharpar, the rivers of Damascus, better than any of the waters of Israel? Couldn't I wash in*

them and be cleansed?' So he turned and went off in a rage. (With a wise appeal) Naaman's servants went to him and said, 'My father, if the prophet had told you to do some great thing, would you not have done it? How much more, then, when he tells you, 'Wash and be cleansed'!" So he went down and dipped himself in the Jordan seven times, as the man of God had told him, and his flesh was restored and became clean like that of a young boy."

I am a Nike woman. Without going into theology and raising the hairs on your neck, I think the easiest way to obey God is to "just" DO IT! That does not mean it IS easy. So many times we see Christians divided over issues God NEVER intended...but Satan certainly thrives on it! I am always quite certain when there are so many fighting over something that it is pretty important. Let me bring up a biggee...baptism. Should we or not? If so, shall we be sprinkled or dunked... how did Jesus do it? Seems pretty simple to me...if I want to be like Jesus, I want to follow in His footsteps. God reminds us in I John 2:6, "Whoever claims to live in Him must walk as Jesus did." Will I understand God's full purpose of baptism? Most likely, not until I see Him face to face in Heaven. Like everything else, we grow as our roots go deeper in Christ. What happens at baptism? So much, but nothing until you DO IT!

I do believe there is MUCH we cannot understand until we take the first step. In Joshua 3, after Moses' death, Joshua is leading the Israelites into the Promised Land. God tells Joshua He is going to exalt Joshua to the Israelites to let them know that God is with Joshua as He was with Moses. In verses 8-17 God says to Joshua, "Tell the priests who carry the Ark of the Covenant: 'When you reach the edge of the Jordan's waters, go and stand in the river'. Joshua said to the Israelites, 'Come here and LISTEN to the Words of the Lord your God. This is how you will KNOW that the living God is among you...as soon as the priests who   carry the ark of the Lord – the Lord of all the earth – set foot in the Jordan, its waters flowing downstream will be cut off and stand up in a heap…Now the Jordan was at flood stage…yet AS SOON AS THE PRIESTS…reached the Jordan and their FEET TOUCHED THE WATER'S EDGE, the water from upstream stopped flowing…and the priests…stood firm on dry ground in the middle of the Jordan…until the whole nation had completed the crossing on dry ground."

God hears us. He wants us to hear Him. He wants us to act on what He tells us, with or without light, with or without understanding. One year Michael and I were at a winter retreat with His House Christian Fellowship in the Upper Peninsula of Michigan. After going to bed very late, we awakened very early to have our quiet time with God. After a time of prayer and Bible reading, we wanted to get out for a little exercise and fresh air…and there is no "fresher" air than the UP's air in the dead of winter! We were way out in the woods and even with all of the snow, it was VERY dark. 'Ole Chicken Butte that I am, I told Michael that this expedition of ours was crazy and we needed to just go back inside – I HATED not being able to see. Instead, I felt God gently say, "Susan, just take the first step." AS I DID, God allowed the moon to shine through the trees for the next step, and the next step, and the next step. When I would stop, so would the light. When I would step forward, the light would shine on my path. I so heard Him singing to me from His Psalms, "My Word is a lamp to your feet and a light for your path (119:105 personalized)…My statutes are wonderful; therefore obey them…the unfolding of My Words give light" (119:129 & 130 personalized).

This teaching has been hugely instrumental in my understanding of God's Word. JUST DO IT! OBEY! Trusting God with whatever He is telling us through His Word, we step forward in obedience. As we step, He sheds light. Too many times I see others waiting to understand. God says obey, THEN you will understand. The more we listen and obey, the more we grow in our knowledge of God and His Word. The more we see Him act on our behalf, the more we come to know we can trust Him…**BECAUSE He said so!**

If you have not caught on by now, Psalms 119 is all about God's Word being living and active in our life…IF we obey! Verses 57–60 says, "You are my portion, O Lord; I have promised to obey Your Words. I have sought Your face with ALL my heart; be gracious to me according to Your promise. I have considered my ways and have turned my steps to YOUR statutes. I will hasten and not delay to OBEY Your commands." WOW! I will hasten and **not delay obeying** – do I hesitate to obey? We have to step out in faith, **BECAUSE HE SAYS SO!**

I want to go back to Naaman and Elisha. Not only does this speak loudly to me about baptism, it SHOUTS to me about obedience and doing things God's way. It made no sense to Naaman that Elisha would have him go to the dirty 'ole waters of the Jordan. It made no sense Elisha would not have him go to a "classier" river and announce Naaman's healing of leprosy to the world. So Naaman went away mad. Thankfully, Naaman had wise servants who reminded him why he had asked Elisha for help. He had leprosy and wanted to be healed. Did it matter where, how, or why Naaman was healed? No, it mattered only that he was healed. So, Naaman needed to do it Elisha's way, because he said so! Could God have healed Naaman of his leprosy in another river? Yes. Could he have healed him by dunking down six times, or two times, or not at all? Yes. But he did not. Can God save us any way He wants to? Absolutely. However, HE CHOOSES a very specific way and if we want salvation, we need to obey, **BECAUSE HE SAID SO!**

Again, I recognize there will be those who will disagree with me. So often we are MUCH MORE concerned about others' feelings and thoughts than we are God's Word. Why do we take those around us much more seriously than we do God? I prefer to have everyone smiling, but if everyone BUT GOD is smiling, I am wrong. I need to step back and see what I have missed…what it is that GOD is saying. I believe it is necessary to take all of His Word to see what He says about salvation, including baptism. Of course I could prove "my point" by choosing certain scripture, just as you could. **OUR** points do NOT matter. **We need ONLY to listen to what God says**. What does He say? I want to encourage you to get in His Word, the Bible. Then, I want you to put blinders and ear muffs on so you ONLY see and hear what God is saying. This is not easy. We have been raised by and exposed to influential people. In many ways, we have been "brainwashed," for good and for bad, to think certain ways; by family, teachers, friends, churches, employers, government, books and life experiences. It is impossible to live and not be prejudiced. I am NOT talking about prejudice toward race or nationality but towards right and wrong. Of course, we think "our way" is right and "their way" is wrong. Is what you have always heard God's way? It needs to be. God is NOT Protestant, Catholic, Anglo-Saxon, Jewish, Black, Male, Female, Southern, Blue Collar, Goth, wearing jeans, shorts or suits. **God is God**. If we choose to believe God, we need to take Him at His Word all of the time, not just when it "feels" good or makes sense. **He is either God all of the time or not at all.**

So what does God declare as His Will? Regarding salvation, I believe He is quite clear that we need to hear His Word, believe His Word, confess our belief in Him as Savior, repent of our sins, and be baptized by immersion. Can God save us any way He wants? Absolutely! But He tells us to do it **HIS** way, **BECAUSE HE SAID SO**! Jesus not only heard and spoke the Word, He IS the Word. He confessed His belief in Himself as the Son of God. Jesus had no sin but took on our sins as the pure Lamb of God, dying on the cross to make a way for us to be one with God. Then He was baptized, to lead us by example in His death (we die to our sins), burial (under the water), and resurrection to new life with His Spirit now within us.

When I was baptized at age eleven, I did so to follow Jesus, **BECAUSE HE SAID SO.** I was questioned about that reasoning later in college, to see if I did it for the right reason. I had to really think long and pray hard for my answer. Did I know then what I know now? No. Do I know now what I will know when I am face to face with Jesus in Heaven? No. But I believe my faith and my reasons were sound: to follow and obey Jesus.

No surprise here. I am not a theologian. I think pretty simply, quite black and white. If Jesus says to do something, I need to do it. Period. I also trust His heart to tell me differently when I am wrong…and He does. I want that. An important analogy for me is that of a child and parent. Suppose I tell my eighteen month old granddaughter, Ellie, to go across the room and bring me "that" ball. I am thinking the blue ball but under the couch, in Ellie's sight, is a pink ball. Ellie runs across the room, gets down on her chubby little knees, reaches way under the couch, grabs the pink ball and runs back to me holding it up so proudly. I know Ellie's heart to obey, to please Grandma. I am not going to spank Ellie for disobeying, I am going to welcome her into my arms with hugs and appreciation. Within her understanding, she obeyed my directions.

As with Naaman, God could have healed him anyway he wanted through Elisha. But He chose a specific way. Although there are times we do not know what to do, God has told us what He does want us to do. Always.

Love one another – John 15: 17, "This is my command: Love one another."

Pray, be joyful, be thankful – I Thessalonians 5: 16-18, "Be joyful always; pray

continually; give thanks in all (not for all) circumstances, for this is the will of Christ Jesus."

Be kind and forgive – Ephesians 4: 32, "Be kind and compassionate to one another, forgiving each other, just as in Christ, God forgave you."

Do not grumble – James 5: 9, "Don't grumble…"

85

Give – Matthew 6: 2, "When you give…" Also, Matthew 6:38, "Give, and it will be given to you. A good measure, pressed down, shaken together and running over, will be poured into your lap. For with the measure you use, it will be measured to you."

Fast – Matthew 6: 16, "When you fast…"

Tithe – Genesis 14: 20, "Then Abram gave him a tenth (= tithe) of everything", (not as much of a command as a principal, reminding us Who owns everything). Ooh, listen to what God says to us in Malachi 3: 8, "Will a man rob God? Yet you rob me. But you ask, 'How do we rob you?' In tithes and offerings." OUCH!

Be Holy (sanctified) – I Thessalonians 4: 3, 7: "It is God's Will that you should be holy (sanctified)…For God did not call us to be impure, but to live a holy life."

How are we doing with all of these? I think we can sum everything up in being holy; loving and praying for one another. I confess one of the hardest ones for me is to forgive someone, when I know I am right. Even worse than that is that God tells us to forgive whether they ever even ask for forgiveness…can you believe that?! How do we know that? Back to Ephesians 4:32, "Forgiving each other, just as in Christ, God forgave you." So a clue here is that Christ died before any of us reading this book were alive. He died for our sins that He knew we were going to commit. God forgave even before we were alive to commit the sin AND to ask for forgiveness! So too, we need to forgive, whether the person who has offended us ever recognizes, admits, and asks forgiveness. Why? **BECAUSE GOD SAYS SO!** I also believe that anger and unforgiveness clogs our spiritual arteries so that we hinder the Holy Spirit from working; we become controlled by our anger rather than being controlled by the Spirit. Anger and unforgiveness eat at us, destroying us more each day we let it rule. God tells us in Colossians 3:15, "**Let the peace of God rule** in our hearts," not anger.

One of my least favorite, but most powerful, verses in the Bible is Romans 12:18, "As far as it depends on you (ME!), live at peace with everyone." EVERYONE! Argh!!! So, when I am angry at my husband (of course, that never happens ;) I need to forgive him, offering him up as a sacrifice to God (sometimes gladly!) and **trusting God to work in his heart** – NOT ME! After 32 years of marriage, as much as I want to "play" the Holy Spirit and tell him what he needs to do or not do, it is ALWAYS much better to quickly forgive him and ask God to "do His thing." Plus, God does a MUCH better job!

There have been times some pretty bad stuff has happened between various people in my life. Many times I did not want to forgive. I did not want to "release" them from my anger as I believed they deserved my wrath. That attitude always hurts God. I feel it is like me driving the nails into Jesus myself. I am choosing to hold onto my anger and not forgive someone for whom Jesus died. I am putting myself on the throne and telling Jesus he was wrong to die for "that" one. Danger!!! Danger!!!

A few times I have found it extremely difficult to forgive. One of those times I felt God asking me if I could trust Him. Could I trust Jesus? "Of course, Lord, but I cannot trust this person." Then God told me I needed to envision Jesus standing between me and the person I was so hurt by and forgive them. I was to trust Jesus, not them. It was a miracle for me. I was able to let go of my anger, hurt, and disappointment because I was entrusting JESUS to deal with it and the person. I could trust Jesus to cleanse my heart of the sin of unforgiveness and free me to love and pray for the other person, as He tells me to do.

God's purpose and will for us to be holy as He is holy is to bring glory to His name. That is why we are created. He wants to reign supremely in our life so others will see Him through our life. He gives us directions on how to do that through His Word. We need to seek Him, listen, and obey. When we do,

His Spirit is able to do **SO MUCH MORE**, "For it is God who works in you to will and to act according to His good purpose" (Philippians 2: 13) "for the praise of His glory" (Ephesians 1: 12, 14). May the following be the goal for our lives to glorify our Savior and Lord!

> *"You are my portion, O Lord; I have promised to obey Your Words. I have sought Your face with all my heart; be gracious to me according to Your promise. I have considered my ways and have turned my steps to Your statutes. I will hasten and not delay to obey Your commands." Psalms 119:57–60*

CHAPTER 11

CHOSEN TO DECLARE HIS PRAISES!

Here I am, sitting in my Michigan State pants, having cheered my team to victory against my Daddy's home state of Tennessee – "we" won by one point – heading on to the Final Four in the March Madness Tournament. I guess my boys forgot to send me the brackets to fill out this year. Can you believe that?!! For the last several years, it has been a tradition in our family to see who GUESSES the best. It is a joke, I know, but a fun one to have them "let" me join in the competition. I do not have a clue what each team's record is, nor do I care. I always vote by default; first MSU or U of M, then a state one of our boys live in, then a school that any of my nephews/nieces went to, then a state where I know someone or have visited, and finally a team who may be an underdog. Funny, I never plan to win but have fared better than a few of my sons who do all the research and take it a little more seriously.

I often marvel at how much time and energy we put into things that really do not matter. I am not saying sports is wrong at all – they can be great fun and super exercise, not to mention a way to build character and camaraderie with others. What does concern me is all the games we play alone, simply for the sake of entertainment. We are going to entertain our-selves to death...and for what purpose?

Many times I find myself asking if something I am about to do is eternally significant. Will it have any effect on my drawing closer to Jesus? Will my efforts affect someone else drawing closer to Jesus? There are many good things in life to do but are they best? Will my choice bring glory to Jesus? As I grow older, I am realizing more and more I have just so much time and energy in each day. I used to feel guilty about that and then I remember (duhh!) that GOD is the One Who gave us 24 hours to each day. I believe Gary Hawes, from Michigan Christian Campus Ministries, aka His House, often said, "God has given us enough time in each 24 hour day to do the per-fect will of God." There is no need to say, "I don't have enough time." We do not have enough time to do what? Our will or God's will? George MacDonald said, "I find the doing of the will of God leaves me no time for disputing about His plans."

God also is the One Who has created my body, allowed it to age and desires to utilize whatever energy I have for Himself. I want my efforts to count for the Kingdom. There are always many well meaning people who want to direct my days for me. When I say no to a good request and see disap-pointment, it used to be a struggle for me. Now I am reminded that I say "No" so I am free to say "Yes" to whatever Jesus has ordered for my day. My goal is to see His smile.

Besides my MSU green/white pants that I am wearing, I am wearing a black sweatshirt with I.N.N.W. engraved on the front that our granddaughter, Sydney, would say, "It don't match." I entered real estate at the peak of the market in January 2005. In the almost four years I worked as a Realtor with Coldwell Banker Hubbell in Lansing, the market went from peak to bottoming out. I believe it was in January 2007 that the Greater Lansing Area Realtors, with my boss and broker, Matt Bowler, as President, initiated **I.N.N.W**. all over the greater Lansing area. It meant, **IF** you are **NOT** going to buy **NOW**, **WHEN**? I am not a bumper sticker kind of person (I do like my little fishy to declare I am a Christian!), but I chose to put the I.N.N.W. sticker in my back window. I did so, not because of real estate, but because it reminded me that **IF I do NOT tell people about Jesus NOW, WHEN will I?** Am I really convinced He is worth talking about, worth living for? Do I truly believe Jesus is the only way to Heaven? Do I care enough for others that I am willing to stand in the gap between them and Hell? Am I willing to risk having someone think I am a goofy Jesus Freak? Heavens to Betsy, YES!! Jesus not only risked His life for that person, He gave His life for that person. For each person! Probably the most memorized verse in all of the Bible is John 3:16, "For God so loved (all of) the world that He gave His one and only Son, that <u>whoever</u> believes in Him shall not perish but have eternal life." Jesus came for ALL!!!

God tells us in I Peter 2:9 that we are "A chosen people, a royal priesthood, a holy nation, a people belonging to God, (so) that you may declare the praises of Him Who called you out of darkness into His wonderful Light." We are here on earth for Him, to sing His praises. My husband, Michael, preached a wonderful sermon this morning regarding the triumphal entry of Jesus into Jerusalem (Luke 19:28–40). The crowds were singing His praises. The Pharisees were not happy about that and told Jesus to tell His followers to be still. Jesus told them that if the people fail to worship, the very stones would cry out His praises. (Michael said this was the beginning of "rock music" ;) This may sound trifle but I NEVER want a stone to have to cry out because I fail to sing my Lord's praises – Heaven forbid!!! That would break my heart because it would break His.

What breaks your heart? Jesus wept over Jerusalem because He knew the hearts of the people. Do we know the hearts of the people around us? Do we care? As Christians, do we believe that God has us exactly where we are to declare His praises? In all we do, we are to praise the One Who has saved us from darkness and rescued us into His Light. Too many times we moan and groan about being useless where we are. Would moving elsewhere or being in a different job make us useful? If we are not useful where we are, how can we be useful where we are not? What we need to do is get our eyes off of ourselves and put them on Jesus, remembering **we are alive to bring glory to HIM!** Do we believe He is worth it? Or are we like the crowd that day in Jerusalem who was cheering for Him only to join the same crowd the next week to shout for His crucifixion? Are we only able to take a stand for Jesus when everyone around us is standing for Him too? Are we a crowd follower, or a Jesus follower? Are committed to Jesus regardless of what those around us are shouting? Are we fickle followers of our Lord? Or are we entirely sold out to Jesus, whatever it takes?

Danny and Kristin were married July 12, 2003. I was told teasingly by one of my dearest friends, Lena Gaines, that I was to wear beige and blend in. She and Bill had already married their first of four sons, Jacob, and had been told that by others. Of course, neither of us were compliant. (I know, surprise there!) Believe it or not, mothers of sons love their children just as much as mothers of daughters. No way did we want to blend in nor take a back seat! We wanted to shout to the world how great our son was and how much we do not like that "leave and cleave" God thing. Our boys always take it seriously and flee the state! Hmmmm! In this case, and with each of our daughters (I don't believe in daughters-in-laws), we are blessed and ever thankful they decided to join our family – especially after getting to know us!

If I am not going to wear beige at my son's wedding, I am not going to wear beige for Jesus! I do not want to blend in! I want people to know I am His and He is mine! I never want anyone to be surprised when they find out I am a Christian. One of my favorite books by Charles Swindoll is <u>Living Above The Level Of Mediocrity</u>. He talks in his forward about his wife, Cynthia, and her unconditional commitment to excellence; an eagle who soars high and loves every minute of it. I highly recommend it for an excellent, challenging read. The chapter titles alone says MUCH about the concise potency of this book:

Confronting Mediocrity:
It Starts in Your Mind
It Involves Another Kingdom
It Costs Your Commitment
It Calls for Extravagant Love.

How Overcoming Mediocrity Means Living Differently:
Vision: Seeing Beyond the Majority
Determination: Deciding to Hang Tough
Priorities: Determining What Comes First
Accountability: Answering the Hard Questions

Confronting Mediocrity Requires Fighting Fiercely:
Winning the Battle Over Greed
Slaying the Dragon of Traditionalism
Removing the Blahs from Today
Becoming a Model of Joyful Generosity

Resisting Mediocrity Includes Standing Courageously:
Standing Alone When Outnumbered
Standing Tall When Tested
Standing Firm When Discouraged
Standing Strong When Tempted

Conclusion: Who's Appraising Your Excellence?

Do any of these chapters strike a note within you, giving you a hunger for more? It is worth every penny and minute spent in reading it. On page 275 Swindoll concludes that "authentic excellence is not a performance…it is there whether anyone ever notices or tries to find out." He goes on to say on pages 277 and 278 "A commitment to excellence is neither popular nor easy. But it is essential. Excellence in integrity and morality as well as ethics and scholarship. Excellence in physical fitness and spiritual fervor just as much as excellence in relationships and craftsmanship. A commitment to excellence touches the externals of appearance, communication, and products just as much as the internals of attitude, vision, taste, humor, compassion, determination, and zest for life. It means **not being different for difference' sake but for God's sake.** After all, He is the One in Whose Book we read, 'If there be any excellence…set your mind on these things' (Philippians 4:8). That's it in a nutshell: A setting of our minds on these things – even if no one else on earth cares or dares."

Even if no one else on earth cares or dares, to see Jesus's smile is enough. If we are involved in the same things that the world is involved in and react the same way, what is going to distinguish "us" from "them?" Why should anyone become a Christian if we look the same as the world? Is there something in us that will draw others to Jesus? Philippians 4:8-9, emphasizes, "Whatever is true, whatever is noble, whatever is right, whatever is pure, whatever is lovely, whatever is admirable – if anything is excellent or praiseworthy – think about such things." If something is not excellent or praiseworthy, don't go there. Choosing to focus on good, positive things helps us focus on God. **By focusing on God with actions that follow, others will see Jesus in us.**

The Book of Esther is another favorite of mine. God shows us a woman and her cousin, Mordecai, who chose to trust God through the roller coaster of their lives. God raised them from poverty to prestige to use them in saving His people of Israel. They were committed to God regardless of whether they perished or not. Esther 4:14 says, "Who knows but that you have come to royal position for such a time as this?"

What about us? Who knows, BUT GOD, if we are where we are "for such a time as this?" I choose to believe my life is in God's hands. IF I am walking in His will, then EVERYTHING that happens is because He has allowed it. Every person I meet is because He has orchestrated it. Every situation I encounter is because He has brought it about, for such a time as this, for HIS PRAISE and GLORY! I do not want to miss anything because my eyes are on myself instead of Jesus!

Are we willing to not blend in with the crowd, not wear beige, so that we stand out for Jesus? Like Swindoll, are we willing to live above the level of mediocrity? Will Jesus spit us out of His mouth because we are lukewarm? In Revelation 3:15-16, Jesus says to us, "I know your deeds, that you are neither cold nor hot. I wish you were either one or the other! So, because you are lukewarm – neither hot nor cold - I am about to spit you out of my mouth." Wow! "I wish you were either one or the other." Either a committed Christian 24/7 (hot) or a non-Christian (cold – corpse). Not a fence sitter. Who do we think we are fooling? Not God!

There is a story about Alexander the Great and a young man who was found scared, deserting from his army. When Alexander came upon him, he asked the young man his name. He replied, "Alexander." Alexander the Great exploded, "Change your ways, or change your name!"

We all know too many church goers who sing God's praises on Sunday only to live like the world the rest of the week. Are we one of them? Does our daily life reflect what we say we believe on Sunday? If we claim to be a Christian, we need to live out what we proclaim or change our name! God wants us living and singing His praises day in, day out. We have been created to be set apart, His royal priesthood, holy nation, just for Him, to sing His praises. Let's live like **WE ARE HIS MUCH MORE!!!**

CHAPTER 12

NAYSAYERS

There always seems to be an Eeyore in every crowd. In fact, it seems as if I am often in the middle of a great day, praising God along the way, and Eeyore steps in. I am assuming here that you all know Eeyore, Winnie the Pooh's friend, who could not see the sun from the shadows? Everything is a shadow for an Eeyore.

I love pointing out God's blessings in our lives and try to focus on the good. There seems to be those Eeyores who take comfort in never being hopeful or seeing the good about a thing. They are easily recognizable; they look as if they have been sucking lemons all day. If I comment on God's beauty of the day, an Eeyore usually replies something like, "Yeah, but you know it can't last." The Eeyores would walk through my door at work and say, "You know if March comes in like a lamb, it is going to go out like a lion…so get ready!" I try to turn it back to enjoying whatever God gives us NOW. The rain looks pretty good after a drought. A cooler, cloudy day is a great excuse to curl up on the couch and read a good book. An Eeyore would say we better watch out for flooding or be careful not to read too much or we will hurt our eyes. Doom and gloom seems to drive them, and Satan wants to take you under with them. Be aware of his tactics.

After years in the ministry, we have learned to love and listen to, but ignore the negativity of the Eeyores. It does not take long for them to show their true colors. If you were to take to heart everything they said, you would not be able to get out of bed in the morning. You would be fearful you might fall and hurt yourself. If you go to work, you might get fired. You would start doubting everyone around you because you would know they really did not like you. It would be obvious to you that people are nice to you only because they are going to expect something from you later on. Your seemingly nice neighbors are telling your other neighbors that your husband goes to work everyday because…well, we all know why! Why? Because he works! Something that has helped us not get consumed by these Eeyores is to say to each other, "Consider the source." What that means to us is to recognize from whence the criticism, fear, or negative talk comes from, and let it go.

I believe God can use criticism from others to help us grow and be even better. So by all means we need to take all criticism to God and have Him weigh it on His scales for us. I ask Him to point His light on what needs to change and blow the rest of the chaff away. I trust Him to do that. I also trust Him to check His Spirit within me and say, "Susan, he/she has a point you need to listen to, even if it hurts." I trust my Potter to shape and mold me. I do not trust the Eeyores in my life. I believe Satan wants to use them to suck us dry, to discourage us from our day, to distract us from God's best. They are energy takers. Michael calls them the "black holes" of society, and shudders. Wikipedia says a black hole "absorbs all the light that hits it, reflecting nothing…it is a region of space from which nothing including light, can escape." A black hole is detected by a conspicuous absence of light, even though it absorbs all the light that hits it, giving back (reflecting) nothing. Know anyone like that? Energy takers. That is why I believe it is important to recognize the Eeyores in our life so we can "consider the source"…and RUN FOR YOUR LIVES!!!

There is a marvelous trilogy, <u>Tales of the Kingdom</u>, <u>Tales of the Resistance</u>, and <u>Tales of the Restoration</u> by David and

Karen Mains that we read aloud to our children at the dinner table or before bedtime. Michael and I liked them as much as the boys. The story line is about children who come to look for the King in their lives...called "sightings." It shares how the people the King puts in our lives to encourage us along the way. He also places people in our lives to protect us and fight with us. Tales draws you into the lives of the various characters and comes alive on paper. Each chapter grows and flows into the next and the next and before you know it you are IN the book, in the family, one of characters.

Naysayers are the Eeyores in our lives. Do you not love that name? Not because it is good, but it is so descriptively poignant. It leaves no doubt with whom you are dealing. They are your discouragers. Naysayers distract you. They zap us of energy and grab the smile out of our hearts. Naysayers drag your heart through the mud and cover the sun with clouds. We need to recognize them for who they are, and what they do in order to diffuse the power they have in our lives.

I used to think I had to be best friends with everyone. Ok, not really, but you know what I mean. It was HUGE for me when I realized not even Jesus was best friends with everyone. Jesus had crowds that followed Him. He had seventy-two trusted disciples whom He sent "two by two ahead of Him to every town and place where He was about to go" (Luke 10:1). He also had an inner circle of twelve apostles with whom He traveled and camped. Yet he also had His favorites, Peter, James, and John. So can I. So can you...AND not feel guilty. Now that does NOT mean we ignore others. Nor does it mean we stop loving and praying for them. But it is okay to recognize there will be those in our lifetime we really do not like. We all know people in our own church we would be happy to introduce to a neighboring church. But guaranteed, once we think we are "escaping" one Eeyore, another one always shows up. Yup! I know! One of the ways I would rationalize every one of our many moves was to think, "At least we won't have to deal with _____." Almost within the week of our move the new Eeyore would show up in living color. YOU fill in the blank. I know you have someone in mind. You are thinking with me right now about that person you see at the grocery store and quickly head down another aisle. Or you see them coming and you turn and bend down to supposedly get something off of the lowest shelf, meanwhile holding a cereal box over your head and a pizza in front of your face. You have probably NEVER done this, but how about the times you see them drive up in your driveway and shout at the kids to turn off the lights and "DUCK!!!" I do believe God intends to use these Eeyores in our lives to transform us into His image by growing us in compassion and teaching us new ways to show them Jesus. God is still working on that "transforming" thing with me.

Sometimes God has placed the Naysayers in our lives for a purpose. Perhaps there is something we may need to learn from them. Think carefully before asking God to remove one from your life. Ask God to order your day to bring in whatever Naysayer He needs to shape us here, mold us there, purify us in His kiln. I have a few I could loan you. Good news. We do not have to have them over for lunch every Sunday, go out with them for fun once a month as it won't be fun, nor vacation with them every summer as you are supposed to look forward to vacations! I also thought I had to give a reason to everyone for everything. My very wise hubby freed me to just say, "Thanks, but I am not able." They do not need to know why. It is not nice to say, "I don't like you." I think we Christians especially give ourselves a hard time about this. We think we are supposed to be nice to everyone. We are. We just do not have to be best friends. Isn't that freeing?!

Try a little test. Listen to yourself. Do you see the good in others or do you only criticize? Are your words uplifting and encouraging or mostly negative? Do you sing "Joyful, Joyful" and frown? Is your favorite fruit a lemon? Would YOU want to hang out with yourself? Why would others?

Are we a Naysayer? Heaven forbid!!! We cannot bring Him praise and glory if all we do is moan and groan and talk about ourselves. He wants us to point to Him! He wants us to be His

Much More. God does not put Naysayers in our lives to make us miserable…we do that well enough by ourselves! He does not plan to throw us little birdies out of His nest so that the big, bad, bully Blue Jays can come and whomp us, stomp us and steal our food. He wants to fill us with His Daily Bread.

God wants us to be His **YAY**sayers! He wants us full of His joy and growing more like Him everyday. Another favorite song is "**Power of Your Love**", **by Geoff Bullock, sung by Hillsong.** It speaks of us coming to God so He can hold, change, renew, surround, and empower us to SOAR with Him day in and day out. God desires for us to have companion "birdies" to soar with through the air, higher and higher…like the geese that honk to encourage the lead bird. He will give us the wind beneath our wings to help us soar like an eagle with Him. God wants **SO MUCH MORE** for us…let Him have it!

CHAPTER 13

JOY BRINGERS

The door opens and in steps a breath of fresh air. The sun bursts on the horizon as she walks through the door. It is as if a new generator has just been switched on and the energy is explosive, energizing all in the room. Everyone smiles and stands to go greet this guest, assured she came for them alone. She hugs this one, that one, calling each by name, lifting spirits with her very presence. Her laughter warms every fiber of the soul and contagiously touches each heart. This is my dear and precious friend, Linda JOY Hanniford. She exemplifies God's intent for us as Christians; to be a Joy Bringer to our world. "The world?!!!" you say, "How does God expect me to do that?!!!" One soul at a time.

Just as we have energy takers in our lives, we have energy givers in our lives. Just thinking of their names brings a smile to our face, a leap in our heart, and a spring to our step. We want to be around energy givers because they bring joy with them. They bring out the best in us. They are happy, positive thinking people who have solutions instead of problems like the Naysayers. Joy Bringers focus on other people. They are the best conversationalists and can talk to and with anyone, always asking questions about that person, their interests while diverting talk about themselves. THEN, they remember whatever has been shared and asks that person the next time they see them; "Hey, how is your church?", "Did Johnny get that job?", "Did Scott sell his house?", "Any of the girls pregnant?", "How many children do you think Danny and Kristin will have?" The answer is, as many as God gives them! Joy Bringers remember because they have been praying.

I believe it was Anne Kelbert at Brighton Christian Church who taught our boys the acrostic for J.O.Y = **J**esus, **O**thers, **Y**ourself. How can you not have joy if you follow this order?

Jesus was a Joy Bringer; crowds followed Him. People sought Him out. He gave them hope. They heard Him gladly. Are you a Joy Bringer? You can be. As Christians, we should be. Who has more hope to share than us? If Christians do not bring joy into a room, who will? I am not talking about being happy all of the time, but if we have Jesus living within us, our countenance should reflect His. His joy should pour out of us, refreshing those around us.

A reminder for me is in <u>God Calling</u> (page 10), "Always, and this daily…we should be channels of Love, Joy and Laughter in His broken world." Channels of love…I really like that. What is even better is that God makes it possible if we allow Him to empty us of ourselves so that His Spirit can fill us, flowing freely through us. Linda JOY Hanniford is one of those channels of love, joy and laughter in this broken world. Linda has struggled with mouth cancer for over 25 years and had several surgeries, never once complaining. She always trusted God to walk with her through each "adventure." I mention this because one specific surgery I had driven to Ann Arbor to be with her and her sisters and went into the waiting room prior to the surgery. I stopped at the desk and told them I was there for Linda Hanniford. The clerk smiled and said, "You and the rest of her 18 best friends! Over there!" Sure enough, there was Linda surrounded by her fan club of cheerleaders and prayer warriors. Why did they each feel they were her best friend? Because she invests her life into them like few others ever do, giving all of her attention to them, knowing their greatest delights and deepest fears. She takes time for people, being a channel of love for God to touch each soul. She sees that as her highest calling in life. Throughout her long battle, she insists she wants to live until she dies. She is. Linda continues to bring joy to the lives of all who know her. Long after Linda is gone, she will live on in the lives of those she touched this side of Heaven.

That will be her legacy...sharing Jesus and His love with everyone who comes along her path so that she can take them with her to Heaven. How about you? How many will meet you in Heaven who say "Thank you, I am here because you shared Jesus and His joy with me?" What will be your legacy? Do you want people to follow in your footsteps? Make sure they are headed in the right direction!

Many people never start living. Others crawl into their own little cocoon and die. God tells us to "Praise the Lord, O my soul, and forget NOT His benefits." (Psalm 103: 2) How do we 'forget not?" We praise the Lord. We get our eyes off of ourselves and on Him. We start counting our blessings, one by one. The following is a great old hymn called **Count Your Blessings by Johnson Oatman, Jr,** 1897. Copyright: Public Domain.

Count Your Blessings

When upon life's billows you are tempest tossed,
When you are discouraged, thinking all is lost,
Count your many blessings, name them one by one,
And it will surprise you what the Lord hath done.

(Refrain)
Count your blessings, name them one by one,
Count your blessings, see what God hath done!
Count your blessings, name them one by one,
And it will surprise you what the Lord hath done

Are you ever burdened with a load of care?
Does the cross seem heavy you are called to bear?

Count your many blessings, every doubt will fly,
And you will keep singing as the days go by. (Refrain)

When you look at others with their lands of gold,
Think that Christ has promised you His wealth untold;
Count your many blessings, wealth can never buy
Your reward in Heaven, nor your home on high. (Refrain)

So, amid the conflict whether great or small,
Do not be disheartened, God is over all;
Count your many blessings, angels will attend,
Help and comfort give you to your journey's end. (Refrain)

I have been privileged to disciple many women over the years. One of the many things I do to encourage them in their walk with God is to have them START counting their blessings. I am always quite surprised how many never even notice God's blessings. So in some ways, they are obeying God to NOT FORGET His many blessings because they do not even know they have them to forget! How sad. Especially as Americans in an affluent society we take our blessings for granted. Wherever you are in America, you are MUCH MORE affluent than the rest of the world! We are a spoiled nation, a selfish generation...and I see it only getting worse. To get our eyes off of ourselves and onto the Great Giver, I suggest making a list of the first 100 blessings for which they are thankful. Too many have looked back at me and said, "100?!!! You have got to be kidding me!" Nope!

Examples flow immediately starting with our five senses and then using each of those sensational senses by recognizing what we "do" with them. Without even trying, I bet you could come up with at least five things for every sense God has given us:

Seeing the faces of our children + four more
Hearing the wind blow in the trees + four more
Tasting Chocolate Moose Tracks ice cream + four more

<u>Smelling</u> fresh mowed grass + four more
<u>Feeling</u> a friend's hand on your shoulder + four more

Right there you have 25 blessings! Then, without thinking, add twenty more "parts" of your body that work; such as knees that bend, legs that support your body, feet without pain, healthy hair, clear breathing, a straight back, etcetera, and you have 45 blessings! You still with me? Now in my case, I think of the family I was born into and all of their spouses and children (13), the family I married into and all of their spouses and children (46), and the family God gave us and their spouses and children (14). I WIN! I count 118!!! The great news is YOU can win too by opening up your eyes to God's many blessings He provides you DAILY!!!!

I believe the biggest hindrance to seeing God's blessings in our lives is US! We think we deserve everything! We are an ego centric being and we expect everyone to know we deserve whatever we want and whatever we get! It does not take long to recognize how blessed we are when you go into a child's ward of a hospital and start looking around. There are ALWAYS other people worse off. Or look at the state of the economy in Michigan right now with 16% unemployment. I thank God I have a job to go to and look at my job as it is, a blessing from God. I do not have to go to work, I get to go to work.

Expectations get in our way. We expect to have a high paying job because we are worth it – who said? We "expect" to live to at least 70 - now in 2010 it is closer to 85 and in western Michigan 95 because we are "preserved" with all of the snow! We tend to say how sad it is if someone dies earlier. For sure, grieving occurs at any age. How often do we ever thank God for the life He gives us, let alone ALLOWS us to live? I have known people who died earlier but lived a far fuller life than those who lived longer and were miserable. Why? **BECAUSE** they breathed each moment for God and brought joy to their "world."

What is your benefit package? Start counting your blessings. Keep adding to your list. Stop taking things for granted. Ask God to open your eyes and heart to Him so that He can point out His many blessings to you. Michigan in the spring has the most glorious hues as the trees and bushes start budding. Every season illustrates God's great beauty! See how God paints you a new picture every day. Listen to the love songs God sings to you through His birds – they are as excited about spring as we are! Feel God's kiss upon your cheek as the wind rushes past you. Breathe in the freshness of the pine trees. Taste God's goodness in His daily provision of your life. God wants to fill us with His joy (Psalms 16:11) so that we can bring SO MUCH MORE joy to our world. Will you let Him?

The best reason EVER to have joy is because **Jesus loves us** and is **THE** Lover of our soul. One of my all time favorite songs is **"Jesus, Lover of My Soul,"** sung by Hillsong (Integrity's Hosanna Music, 1992). This song reminds us how MUCH we need Jesus and how MUCH we need to seek Him as our very closest friend, truly our **JOY BRINGER!!!**

~~~Special Note~~~

Linda JOY Hanniford awoke to real life when she looked up into the face of Jesus as He held her in His eternal, loving arms July 8, 2010. Once again, she is able to speak her marvelous words of love and is free of pain, celebrating SO MUCH MORE the new life God has given her! See you in the morning, Dear Friend! You shall be forever loved!

CHAPTER 14

ATTITUDE OF GRATITUDE

"Give thanks in all circumstances, for this is God's will…"
I Thessalonians 5:18

Thankfulness is not natural. It needs to be taught, caught and regularly modeled. To tell your children to SAY "please and thank you" is pretty much useless unless they hear you saying it. It seems as if thankfulness is becoming a lost "art." Not many are looking for it. I understand this in the secular world; they do not know Jesus. I do not understand it in the Christian world. We are the ones who say we know the Giver of all life, and sing the Doxology by Thomas Ken, 1709, Copy Right: Public Domain.

> "Praise God from Whom all blessings flow;
> Praise Him, all creatures here below;
> Praise Him above, ye heavenly host;
> Praise Father, Son, and Holy Ghost."

We also are the ones who sing, "Standing on the Promises" while sitting on our hands in the pews. Or "Joyful, Joyful, We Adore Thee" with naught a fraction of a smile upon our lips. Is this joy? What about "I Surrender All" as we hoard our time and belongings. God Calling (April 6) says, "So often man, crying out for some blessing, has yet such tight hold on some earth-treasure that he has no hand to receive Mine, as I hold it out in Love." I believe God gives to us so that we can pass it on to those around us; our goods, our love, our joy, our attitude of gratitude. God wants us to be His channel of love to a dying world. What is different about us? Nothing, if we are impolite, or if we moan and groan like everyone else. Not only do we NOT thank people for acts of kindness and service, we never offer a hand to help. Last week I was contacted by someone who said I was too loud in the kitchen. I was cleaning up their mess and they couldn't concentrate on the Bible Study. I won't tell you what I wanted to say. I have learned it is best if I do not respond right away with my reactions. It is also best for those to whom I am reacting. God, in His time, can work miracles. I spoke with this person a week later and told them I was sorry for being noisy and IF there is a next time, feel free to come to me and we can quietly clean up together!

We have had numerous people over for meals and to spend the night. I am probably NOT a servant (guess it is pretty evident) because it bugs me when they sit around watching me work and never offer to help. THEN, in the morning after a good night's sleep, shower, and breakfast, I am stunned by their lack of appreciation when they leave. Guess they think they deserve it! Guess they also thought I was their maid so felt free to leave towels all over their bathroom and bed totally unmade and, one time, snotty 'ole Kleenexes in several places of the room, including the floor. Maybe they did not see the waste basket. Hmmm. Hmmm again. I try to say "hmmm" when I am flabbergasted! I do not serve to be appreciated, but am probably just too attuned to their lack of appreciation. If they had been my children, I would have said, "'Scuse me, Mister, get back here and clean up this room!" Or, "Hey Buddy Boy, bring your plate over here." If I got any lip (they knew better) then they could clean up all the dishes. Where do our adults come from? From children who were never taught thankfulness or how to have a heart attitude of gratitude. However, I do not believe in forever blaming parents. As adults ourselves, we need to recognize what we may be lacking and START **now** to live right, in every area of our lives. We are responsible for who and what we become – and our attitude about life!

Martha Washington said, "I have learned that the greater part of our misery or unhappiness is determined not by our circumstances but by our disposition." Amen! My minister growing up at Emmanuel Baptist Church in Pontiac, Michigan was Tom Malone, a great preacher and man of God. He would often comment in a nasally tone on this person or that person moaning and groaning, "Well, under the circumstances..." He would quickly respond, "We are not to be 'under the circumstances' but be overcomers." Dr. Malone would then quote I John 5:4-5, "This is the victory that has overcome the world, even our faith. Who is it that overcomes the world? Only he who believes that Jesus is the Son of God." Back to focus! Eyes off of self and onto Jesus – it is in Him we have the victory and can live a victorious life! Our choice! Then Dr. Malone would have his wife, Joyce, start us singing a good 'ole Baptist hymn. Actually, I do not know or care if it is a Baptist hymn, but for sure it is a song of praise to Jesus! This may rattle some of your cages but I believe **God calls us to Himself**, His CHURCH, not a specific denomination. I see myself as a Jesus follower!

Victory in Jesus
By Eugene Monroe Bartlett, 1939
Copy Right: Public Domain

I heard an old, old story, how a Savior came from glory,
How He gave His life on Calvary, to save a wretch like me;
I heard about His groaning, of His precious blood's atoning,
Then I repented of my sins, and won the victory.

Chorus
O victory in Jesus, My Savior, forever.
He sought me and bought me, with His redeeming blood;

He loved me ere I knew Him and all my love is due Him,
He plunged me to victory, beneath the cleansing flood

I heard about His healing, of His cleansing power revealing.
How He made the lame to walk again and caused the
blind to see;
And then I cried, "Dear Jesus, come and heal my
broken spirit,
And somehow Jesus came and brought to me the victory.
(Chorus)

I heard about a mansion He has built for me in glory.
And I heard about the streets of gold beyond the crystal sea;
About the angels singing, and the old redemption story,
And some sweet day I'll sing up there the song of victory.
(Chorus)

Attitude can make or break you. Our choice. What else explains my attitude on my birthday for the last 56 years? I CHOOSE to wake up happy, excited about the day all about me! No matter what happens, my attitude is a good one – how can it not be when you have phone calls of love, a smothering of mail with birthday wishes, and piles of presents?!!! How about sunny days compared to dreary days? Why are we more upbeat and positive on sunny days than we are on dark days? It is not just about Vitamin D from the sun, it **IS** about **CHOOSING** the right attitude!

Our son, Danny, and his precious wife, Kristin, are spectacular parents and they have the three most marvelous girls. For those of you who may be grandparents, you will understand this. One of my very favorite things about having grandchildren is watching our children parent and be uncles. Our boys are THE best, as are their wonderful wives at being great aunts! I always teased Danny, our "macho" son, that he was going to end up with girls. I think I enjoy this irony as much as God does ;) Of course, we KNOW God knows what is best for us (as He did with us and our five sons) and praise Him daily for these little girls. They are now expecting number four so we are eager to meet this precious "gift." Sydney JOY is five, Madeline GRACE is three, and Elisabeth HOPE is eighteen months. Each is "practically perfect" in every way and we delight in them! After raising five boys, I thought girls would be easier. Sydney, Maddie, and Ellie have got the energy of their Daddy, the feistiness of their Mommy, AND the emotions of GIRLS – can you believe it?! The reason I bring this all up is because in their parenting, often Kristin and Danny will say to the girls, "Change your attitude." I used to think that was a little funny to hear when their little hearts were breaking and tears were flowing. However, I also believe parents know best WHEN they are seeking God in the "How To's" of raising their children. Sure enough, when the girls are truly hurting, tenderness galore comes from their parents, even Danny. When tears are flowing because of a bad attitude, usually selfishness, Danny and Kristin are so very wise to check their children's motives right away. This teaches the girls that they are in charge of their attitude. NOW is the time to shape and mold those attitudes. What is extra cute is when I hear Sydney or Maddie tell Ellie or one another, "Better change your attitude." ☺

If I can become half the woman my Mom was, I will be thrilled and others will be blessed. Not only did Mom teach us manners but she modeled them. I have heard it said you learn the true nature of a person playing Monopoly with them. I have witnessed seemingly kind people throwing the board if they lose. Team sports are another way to meet the "real" person…scary! For years I had also heard you see the authentic person if they get Alzheimer's or Dementia. My Mom had always been the healthiest person I knew. She ate right, exercised regularly, and never drank or smoked. Dad died in August of 1993.

In March of 1995, Mom started having shortness of breath. She had been in Florida since Christmas. Concerned for her health, Scott flew down earlier than normal to drive her home. Tests showed she needed to have open heart surgery to replace her mitral valve. Surgery was done in April and as awful as that was, she recuperated wonderfully. One month later, Kaye, and her daughter, Whitney, were home visiting and out to dinner with Mom and Scott. Mom had a stroke. Most likely from the surgery, she shot a clot to the brain. I received "the" call in Lansing, jumped in the car, rushing to St. Joseph Hospital in Pontiac, about 1 ½ hours away. My heart was racing the whole time. When I arrived at the hospital, Mom was okay but very confused. Her speech was not clear. She had several more tests. The next day they sent her home with speech and occupational therapy to follow. She needed someone with her. My family is great! We all helped but the majority of the responsibility fell on Patti and her family. We will be forever grateful. Mom made some progress, but it was slow. Her left side had been weakened but she regained her strength in her legs and arms. Then she had another stroke. In July we were back in the hospital with several more tests in which they discovered a brain aneurysm. The first of August, two years after our Dad had died, Mom underwent brain surgery. During the surgery and shortly thereafter, she suffered two more strokes. Recovery was neither easy nor very successful.

We were quite discouraged, as was Mom. Yet, despite all these changes for her, she continued to trust God and thank Him. She thanked us for her care, for our time, for our love. As the result of her many strokes, Mom acquired what they call Multi-Infarct Dementia. The Mayo Clinic Family Health Book (page 518) describes it as "A step-by-step loss of memory, marked by clouding of consciousness at each step; disintegration of personality with increasing depression, with abrupt change in mental state." My Mom had never been depressed a day in her life. This was such a loss for both her and us. Saddened, we watched our Mom disappear. In many ways, she "died" two years before she physically died on July 20, 2005. The last ten years of her life, despite the many disappointments and losses, Mom still displayed a heart attitude of gratitude. Though her speech was diminished, she never ceased to say THANK YOU. Her greatest disappointment, besides not being able to drive anymore to visit her friends and go shopping, was losing her ability to read. She was an avid reader and dearly missed being able to read her wonderfully worn-out Bible every morning. Yet His Word lived within her. She never forgot her Father and He never forgot her. She continued to pray. Later, we found her prayer lists in her Bible. Many words were no longer recognizable words. Nevertheless, Mom would lift them up to God, confident He would know what she meant, and for whom she meant them. She continued to praise Him, thanking her God.

Up until the last two years of her life, she continued to send cards to family and friends to encourage them, even though her words were nonsensical. The last year we finally had to surrender her to an Alzheimer/Dementia home for her care. We hated that. Even though she did not know us, we still knew her. We felt we had given up on our Mom. Yet, she would have been the first to say it was time. As she grew weaker and more confused, she spoke less and less. Still to each and every caregiver, she said THANK YOU. Her heart remained His, He remained hers. She was forever grateful.

I believe one of the major reasons Jesus told us to serve one another is to get our eyes off of ourselves. I confess that I struggle with depression at times, the "woe is me" syndrome. Not always is it due to my own selfishness, but sometimes because I have been hurt by someone; whether intentionally on their part or from being too sensitive myself. Upon occasion it is because I am so very sad for someone else hurting due to whatever is happening in their life: illness, loss of job, marriage problems, heart break over children's choices, death. I do not know of a better way to correct my own attitude or depressed heart than to get outside of myself and do something for someone else. First I call out to Jesus and repent of my selfishness, if that is the case. I ask Him to help me get my eyes off of myself and onto Him, to help me have a "heart attitude of gratitude." Then I will ask Him to direct me to whom He would have me reach out to, whether by phone, card, email, or visit. It is amazing to me how quickly His SONshine comes into my heart when I empty it of me and make room for Him.

I am His and He is mine. How can we as Christians NOT be thankful for Jesus? How can we NOT have a heart attitude of gratitude for all He is? All we are is because of Him. What more do we need? I think many Christians have too small of a view of God. Their god must be a small god because they keep losing him. Many have him all figured out. They keep him safely in the little box they make up for him so they can get him off of the shelf whenever they need him. One of my favorite writers, Max Lucado, in his book, <u>Fearless</u> speaks of boxes in his book (164, 165):

> "Boxes bring wonderful order to our world. They keep cereal from spilling and books from tumbling. When it comes to containing stuff, boxes are masterful. But when it comes to explaining people, they fall short. And when it comes to defining Christ, no box works. Box-sized gods. You'll find them in the tight grip of people who prefer a god they can manage, control, and predict. This topsy-turvy life requires a tame deity, doesn't it? In a world out of control, we need a god we can control."

THE God is not in a box. God is the CREATOR of boxes **AND** everything in and around them! Luke 1:37 says, **"NOTHING is impossible with God!"** Get that? **NOTHING!** That pretty much includes everything! Everything!

Better than even Max Lucado, listen to what God says in Romans 11: 33 – 36:

> *"Oh, the depth of the riches of the wisdom and*
> *knowledge of God! How unsearchable His judgments,*
> *and His paths beyond tracing out! Who has known the*
> *mind of the Lord? Or who has been His counselor?*
> *Who has ever given to God, that God should repay*

him? For from Him and through Him And to Him are ALL things. To Him be the glory FOREVER!"

Our attitude is our choice. God tells us that "Your attitude should be the same as that of Christ Jesus" (Philippians 2: 5). I think we all have a way to go. I know I do. If our attitude IS our choice, let us make it one of gratitude. There is SO MUCH MORE God desires for us if we open ourselves to Him and His ways, praising and thanking Him daily with a heart attitude of gratitude.

Our son, Steve, shared with me the song, **"Satisfy" by 10th Avenue North**. It is a perfect song to help us check our attitude of gratitude. It reminds us to refocus our minds and hearts with thankfulness, praising God for being **SO MUCH MORE** than ALL that we could ever hope or imagine!

CHAPTER 15

GOD INCIDENTS

*"It is God who works in you to will and to act
according to His good purpose." Philippians 2:13*

*"You ought to say, if it is the Lord's will,
we will live and do this or that." James 4:15*

I was backing out of the garage the other day and had a
strong pressure on my right shoulder and turned my head
to the right and slammed on my brakes! Our #3 car was right
behind me! Many would say that was a CO-incident. I call
it a GOD incident! I stopped because God stopped me. The
not so funny thing is that every morning as Michael leaves
for work I remind him about the car being back there...then
I forget! That is called payback! I call it our #3 car because
although we own it, we let Matt use it whenever he is home for
work or outings. With him away at college this past year, we
gave it to Steve and Emily in Iowa to use for the winter. They
had returned it just the week before and we were "re"learning
that it was there. Guess I am a slow learner ☹

We are a little extra sensitive to cars in our driveway. We
like them and all that but they remind us of another incident
ten years ago...I do not think God was in that one. It was our
youngest son, Matt's, 10th birthday and we were rushing off

in our full sized van the boys called "The Chick Mobile." We were going bowling with all of the boys and Matt's best friend Mike Snyder. Michael was driving and somehow accelerated that old van up to 60 mph in 3 seconds (okay, a little exaggeration, it could have been 4 seconds) and we slammed full force into our eldest son, John's, newly bought, with his own money, used-to-be cute Grand Am. We all were sick. Okay, not all of us. Danny, Steve, and Josh were laughing, which did not help. Matt was crying. John was crying. Poor Mike Snyder did not know what to do. I felt horrible for John. But we were on a mission of FUN so after looking at the damage, got back in the van and took off for a jolly round of bowling. Needless to say, Matt was not in a hurry for another party.

I do not believe in co-incidents. Most people do. You hear it all of the time. "What a co-incidence!" "Listen to this amazing co-incident!" I choose to believe that my life has a much higher power overseeing my life than some little "co-incident." I do not believe in "chance" meetings. Our friend, Dean Trune, calls them "divine appointments." That sounds much more heavenly to me and reminds me to Whom I have surrendered my life. I do believe in a God Who is able, **MUCH MORE than able**, to orchestrate every happening in my life. NOT like a puppet, but as a caring Father. I also prefer to give Him ALL of the credit for whatever occurs in my life. I trust Him.

You see, IF I am walking in the perfect will of God, then whatever happens, He has allowed. Nothing can "get" to me without His permission. So, if I sit by someone on a plane who is a mother of young boys, I recognize God probably has a higher calling for my time than to talk about the weather or read a favorite magazine. I call that a GOD incident (or divine appointment). In fact, whomever I sit by, I know He has plans to be lifted up. Do I always know what to say? Heavens, no! So I ask Him. I confess there are times I am extra tired, or selfish, and request that I get to fly "solo," without a seat mate. Sometimes God says yes and sometimes He says no. Whenever He says "no," I get ready for a God incident – not necessarily great but definitely an adventure. Sometimes God throws one of "those" Eeyores my way just to see if I have learned anything. I almost can hear Him chuckling. I ALWAYS know He wants me to learn more about Him, others, and myself…and see Him "do His thing."

Now if I am NOT walking in God's will, I have no guarantees. Can God still orchestrate incidents? Absolutely! Can God rescue me if I get myself in trouble?

Positively! We all know that we have done dumb things that could have hurt ourselves and/or others and we were spared. By chance? WHO IS CHANCE?!!! NO, by God!

Shamefully, the main reason I drive the speed limit is to be protected under God's will as He tells us to obey the laws of our land. Simply to obey should be my reason. I am working on that. Years ago I realized that if I get in an accident with the boys because I am speeding, I am responsible for whatever happens. I could not bear the thought of injuring one of our boys. If I get in an accident while obeying God's laws, then I am in His will, and for whatever reason, He has allowed it. Could God get me through the crisis either way, yes, but how MUCH MORE I would struggle to forgive myself if I were responsible. God never intends us to go through many of the heartaches that we bring on ourselves.

Thankfully, nothing happened but I risked our boys lives and my own one time in the name of "fun." Please do not report this to the Mason Police…and I am not sure I have ever told Michael this either…hmmm. One day I was driving all five boys down a country road in Mason in our Chick Mobile when a huge John Deere combine came over a hill towards us. Given, we had lots of room before impact. BUT, I thought it would be fun to drive on the other side of the road playing CHICKEN with the combine. The boys were in Heaven (well, almost) laughing hilariously and cheering me on, chanting, "Chicken!!! Chicken!!! Go Mom!!!" What a cool Mom, eh? NO!!! Thanks to God, I came to my senses and jerked the wheel over to my lane. The severity of my "play" hit me. My brainlessness could have gotten all of us killed. My choice to get outside of God's will by breaking the law and driving on the wrong side of the road could have ended in fatality. God was gracious. God is always gracious. But often things happen because we choose to be stupid.

When we moved to Kalamazoo in the fall of 2008, I took a couple of months off from working. I like not working. However, I also knew this was THE time like no other for me to chip in with a little extra money to go towards Matt's college. I also wanted the luxury of going back and forth to see our precious granddaughters in Florida. Within a couple of months, I started looking for jobs. I had thoroughly enjoyed real estate in Lansing but the market was very difficult and I did not know the area well enough nor have many contacts. Could God still work through me as He did in Lansing? Yes! So I told Him I was open to real estate but asked Him to show me if there was another job he wanted me to look into. He reminded me I had always loved being around old people – and again, there is no place like Kalamazoo to find OLD people because of how all that snow preserves them – up into their 90's and even some 100's!!!! Amazing! So I put out feelers for a Care Giver position and searched all of the want ads online and in the paper. I even put an ad in the paper as a Care Giver. God gave me a job with Leonard, a brilliant 90 year old man who just needed me to come and sit with him while his daughter got a little respite for herself. It was easy and wonderful, but not enough hours. I went to Senior Day Expo with about 80 different vendors trying to solicit the business of senior citizens for Respite Care. There I was in the midst of all these "older than me" people. It is a great way to feel young! I met many business directors and turned in my newly made business card and resume' to several. I would stop and talk and ask if they were hiring. Many senior services were looking for Care Givers. It just so happened (**No! GOD happened!**) that one of the places had just started looking for an administrative assistant. Hmmm. Interesting. Co-incident? No! **GOD INCIDENT!!!** I applied and went in for the interview the next week. I was offered the job and, crazy me, thanked them but said I was hoping for something a little closer to home and for more money.

Hope away, Girlfriend!!!! My pride took over and I passed up a REAL job – in the midst of Michigan's awful economy! Not only that but about two weeks later, Leonard was getting stronger and did not need me anymore – argh!!! Now what? God is what!!! So back to the Want Ads. Nothing. Michael and I had gone to a funeral of one of our friend's parents and afterwards I noticed I had gotten a message on my phone. Calling back right away, I found it was Park Village Pines, the Christian Assisted Living Residence who had kindly offered me a job. The girl they had hired had found another job full time so they wanted to know if I might be interested. This time I said yes! One look from Michael confirmed my thoughts; God wanted me there. We had prayed for God to not only close, but nail shut, any doors He did not want me to go through and swing wide the one He did want for me. God knew I was a little slow so He made it easy…one door…open! I stepped through!

The first day of work was heavenly! Not only was I surrounded by old people (our son, Josh, calls them Prunies ;) but it was a true Christian atmosphere with the Director and Managers all being on the same page AND in the same Book, God's Word! It got even better! In walks one 98 year old woman who instantly says, "Oh my!!! YOU are beautiful!!!" Wow! THIS IS HEAVEN…or make believe! I laughed and said thank you. She took off her glasses, wiped them, and in the next breath said, "I can't see a lick anymore!" Again, a chuckle from God ☺ What a great sense of humor our God has!!!

I have a new friend, Aline, I met last fall at a women's retreat for which I was speaking on the Joy of the Lord and Day By Day Mentoring. God engineered the meeting. Aline was seeking the Lord and His joy and desired to be mentored…she did not know it yet, but she was. God knew it. The retreat was in Battle Creek but we both live in Kalamazoo. Hmmm. We became friends. She started regularly attending our church. We are now able to get together twice a month to grow in our friendship and in our Lord. **GOD INCIDENT!** Why

NOT give Him the credit? It is so very helpful to me to recognize and acknowledge God's active working in my life.

Aline has been growing in her love for the Lord. She is having a daily quiet time with God in prayer and His Word, growing by leaps and bounds. Two weeks ago she got a job at Park Village Pines as a Care Giver. Yesterday one of our dear saints was dying and the family wanted someone with him 24/7. Aline was asked if she would be comfortable sitting in Don's room with him. She heartily agreed. Don asked if she would be willing to read from the Bible to him – specifically Psalms and Proverbs. So all afternoon Aline read to Don and cared for him – they even prayed together. Is that not amazing how things like that just happen? **GOD HAPPENS!**

God was gracious in every way when he created our boys. We knew without a doubt they would all be hairy (I have been accused of being a Hobbit – hairy feet and love to stay home) and need glasses. We did not know how well they would fare with brains. Again, God was gracious. None of our boys went to our school, Michigan State, (Go Green!) when they went to college. John went to Central Michigan University in Mt. Pleasant and got actively involved in His House (aka Michigan Christian Campus Ministries). John grew wonderfully in the Lord, made some great friends and even lived in the guys' house there on campus. We are forever thankful for the ministry MCCM provides to students on secular campuses.

When it came time for Danny to go to college, nowhere else did he want to go but the University of Michigan. He applied to three schools. He prayed. We prayed. We again asked God to nail shut any doors He did not want Danny to walk through and to swing wide the door He did want for him. Danny is as smart as any of the boys and probably one of the hardest workers but struggled more with testing. He did well on the ACT but not as high as U of M usually requires so we were not real hopeful. The odds (who are the odds?!!!) and statistics were against him. God was for him. He got in. He did well. Romans 8: 31, **"If God is for us, who can be against us?"** powerfully came to mind.

Despite our concerns about Danny going to a very liberal school, it was obvious God wanted Him there. He grew him by leaps and bounds spiritually and gave him many Godly friends. I know there are many of you who probably disagree with us letting our boys go to secular schools. That is okay, they are our boys, not yours. We have continued to look to God to grow our boys and He has been ever faithful. We are all for wherever GOD wants our children…and yours. We are cautious to listen for HIS voice and look for HIS smile, not that of the world or even other well meaning Christians or family members. We are accountable to Him. If all of us Christians went to Christian schools and hid out in our churches, how would the world ever know about Jesus? God commissions us to "go into all the world," not stay. If we are the "salt of the earth" and "light of the world" (Matthew 5: 13, 14) how will the world taste and see IF we are not living among them?

Steve probably had the highest grade point average and did well on the ACT. He, too, applied to the University of Michigan and two other schools. He prayed. We prayed. Nail shut, swing wide. Shockingly, U of M did not admit Steve. He was crushed. We were crushed for him. Calvin College, an excellent Christian college in Grand Rapids, had been diligent pursuing Steve for soccer. The week he was rejected at U of M, Calvin College approached him again. Strangely, we had never considered a Christian school. Did God have to close the doors to U of M to get us to consider Calvin? We were not even open to it before. Nailed doors can be answers to our prayers when we trust God with the leading. They can help redirect our attention to something or someone who had been invisible. Co-Incident? **GOD INCIDENT!!!**

By the time Josh was ready to go to school, his heart was headed for Calvin. He had been there to visit Steve and liked what he saw. We liked what we saw in Steve and his friends. We were impressed with the professors who become friends with the students. Josh, too, applied to three colleges. He prayed. We prayed. He was accepted at all three colleges. Sometimes I think God says, "You pick." I do know that God's desire always is wherever we go, whatever we do, to bring glory to His name. Josh does.

Last, but not least, Matt prepared to graduate from Grand Ledge High School. We all thought he would be going to Calvin also. All except Danny (and God). He applied to three colleges. He prayed. We prayed. He, too, was accepted at all three. Matt enjoyed his visits with Josh and Steve at Calvin and was impressed with what he saw for himself at Fridays at Calvin, a one day orientation. We also liked the idea of Calvin because it would be closer to us once we moved to Kalamazoo than Ann Arbor. He was headed for Calvin…or so we thought. Danny (and God) had other ideas. Coincidently (or was it a **GOD INCIDENT**? I was not sure at the time), Danny just "so happened" to have a business trip scheduled in Ann Arbor. He, Kristin, Sydney, and Maddie flew up to stay with us in Lansing and then Dan drove to Ann Arbor for the week. Wednesday he called us to see if we could come down to meet him for dinner; he missed his girls. We, of course, said yes. After a delicious dinner, Danny asked if we would be willing to walk around campus for some fresh air and more time for him with the girls. Yes. Then it happened. It all became vividly clear. As his arm slithered around Matt's shoulders and he started pointing here and there, we saw the future unfold before our eyes. I wanted Calvin, I felt "safe" at Calvin. Then Dan really "cheated" because he took us to the splendidly collegiate, better than Ivy League, Law Quad. Poor Matt. He was torn. To please Mom or Danny? Or God? Hmmm. I voted for MOM! God continued to work on all of our hearts. Again, that 'ole familiar question He often asks me, "Susan, do you trust me?" But God…he is my "baby." But God…he is on meds for his seizures. But God…he has never been away from me for any length of time, what if he has a seizure? But God…we KNOW Calvin is "safe," U of M is sooooooo liberal. I felt God peeling back my hands, my grip on Matt. He ever so gently reminded me (again) that HE had NEVER been away from Matt and NEVER would be. "Susan, you have to let ME shape and mold Matt MY way, not yours. I have big plans for him and I need him at U of M." OK. What else do you say to God? Coincident to have Danny come home? **GOD INCIDENT!** Danny got to be a part of God's planning. After all, Danny had prayed Matt into existence – yes, it was Danny who had asked God for another little brother. Guess Danny and God have been partners for awhile!

Matt not only went to U of M in the fall of 2008 but went a week EARLY ☹ to help with Move-IN Makers, meeting and moving in new students. HE was a new student and already reaching out. He is probably our most social and they are all amazing when it comes to people! At orientation and in that first week, he met some awesome friends – CHRISTIAN friends! He continues to meet people all the time and has a CORE group of about 20 strong Christian friends – at a secular college!!! In fact, Matt got involved in a campus church right away, began doing Young Life at one of the local high schools, and will be an R. A. (Resident Assistant) next year in his junior year. Hmmm. Yup! Guess God knows what He is doing. Pretty good planning God...okay, and Danny.

Start looking for God's fingerprints each day, every day, throughout your life. Hebrews 4:12 tells us He is "living and active" in our lives. Put your Super Sleuth hat on. See Him working, guiding, directing, leading, pushing, and pulling. **GOD INCIDENTS** are **MUCH MORE** than mere coincidence. They are God showing us intimately and personally that He wants to be actively involved in our very lives!

HE IS ALIVE and SO MUCH MORE than we ever hoped or imagined, worthy of all our praise and glory!!!

CHAPTER 16

HELP ME SHOW YOU OFF, LORD!

"Let your light shine before men, that they may see
your good deeds and praise your Father in Heaven."
Matthew 5: 16

Remember Show and Tell in school? I used to love to take in my favorite stuffed animals and tell my many stories about them. When you grow up in the country, your imagination grows rampant so you always have lots of stories to tell. They may not be real but they were good! I played pretty much with just my brother, Scott, who is four years older than me. Bobby Grant from next door would often be part of our "gang" and he was six years older, my sister Kaye's age. Yes, I was a tomboy. I preferred to be outside. If Scott and Bobby were too cool for me, I would wander inside looking for my younger sister, Patti. We would play with our Barbies and Kens. We both had one of each – who needs more than that?!! I never really liked them because I thought their bodies were ugly... remember, I was about 8! Then I really did not like my Barbie once Patti cut off her hair. Usually Patti was upstairs in her room playing school with her stuffed animals. She even had lunch, recess, and if they were bad, you would see them sitting out in the hall. Back then, "bad students" could actually be disciplined! Look out! Patti knew how to control her class! I do not remember playing much with Kaye. It seems as if she was usually in her room reading.

My favorite Show and Tell was when I could get my Dad to come into our classroom. I wanted all the kids to see how handsome he was. I wanted them to know he owned a business, was in politics, taught Sunday School and was the BEST DAD IN THE WHOLE WIDE WORLD! When you are proud of someone, you want to show them off!

I am proud of Jesus! As a young Mom, I was always busy with the boys. I wanted to incorporate into our days ways that we, as a family, could show off Jesus! Michael worked lots of hours and I wanted to fill our days with play that would honor Jesus, to see Him smile. Showing off Jesus became my goal for me and the boys. I wanted it to be as natural as breathing in both work and play. I never wanted anyone to question whether or not we were Christians. Not because we were weird (which we were…okay, are) but because they saw Jesus in us, day in and day out.

Chris Rice speaks of being a candle to our world in his song, **"Go Light Your World."** This song wonderfully reminds us of our responsibility as Christians to be lights in a dark world. We also need to seek out those who are hurting and confused so that the fire God has lit within us by His Spirit may light up and warm their world as well.

We have always lived in awesome places with the best neighbors ever! God has always provided us with young families with kids for our boys to play with and older people for us to adopt and love on. Perfect blending! God is so good – all the time! Before Michael and I were married, we had shared with God our desire to have me be able to stay home once we had children. God honored that prayer. So to honor Him, I designated myself the Neighborhood Welcoming Committee and the Kool-Aid House for all the kids to come and play. My "committee" was the boys! We would make and bake cookies to welcome new neighbors, arrange for meals to be taken in to sick ones or those with new babies. Michael made up a great neighborhood directory with the layout on one side and names, addresses, and phone numbers on the other side. We wanted everyone to know everyone! I also would type up little newsletters about quarterly to update everyone and would ask for any prayer requests, and let them all know we were praying daily for them. Some responded positively, others did not respond. That was okay. I did not do it for them, I did it for Jesus! I wanted God to be free to use us however HE needed to touch the lives of those He placed around us. Overall, I think it was only good because it united our neighborhood and we were often asked when the next quarterly update was coming out, or if we had an extra directory because they had misplaced theirs. No better way to learn names of people than to pray for them daily!

My reason to be the Kool-Aid house was selfish. I wanted to know everyone our boys were playing with and everything that was happening. Steve calls me "Snoops" but I call it Mother's Prerogative! I also knew some of the Moms were not always home when they said they would be, and some of them were pretty much useless even if they were home. You have heard of DD? Designated Driver? I was DM for Designated Mom. Of course I was the one who did the "designating" but I am pretty sure I saw God's nod of approval and Jesus' smile. That was good because I needed Him to participate...DAILY!!! Remember, I had FIVE boys!!! I still do – God did a great job!

Another HUGE plus in having everyone at your house is that you get to make the rules AND carry them out. Everyone knew our rules: be nice to each other, no swearing, and I WAS IN CHARGE! I would always give warnings, but if they chose not to do it my way, they were sent home. That did not keep them away. They would always return the next day. I am not sure they had enough fear of ME! Our next door neighbor had two boys the age of our oldest boys. Their youngest one was a MONSTER! When I first started doing this, there were days I would see him coming and drop to the floor and loudly whisper for the boys to HIDE!!! One day Michael was home and this occurred. He asked me why I was doing that. I told him. He laughed and pulled me off of the floor, opened the door, and told the little boy our children would be playing by themselves for now – and to go home. He did! Michael then pulled rank as "Director of the Kool·Aid House" and reminded me I was the adult, and that I never had to have any child control my day. You cannot imagine how freeing that was for me. Even though I was a little embarrassed that I had let a six year old scare me, I regained my composure and remembered how to flex my "Mom muscles," also known as God-given authority. God had given us our boys, our house, and the authority to best care for them.

No better way to share Jesus than through relationships! Day in, day out exposure to people helps them come to know that you care for them and they open up. Moms would come over to visit while their kids were playing. They would open up about themselves. Kids would share things (if the parents only knew!) that gave us insight into how to best pray. We prayed. God worked. We have been blessed to know neighbors who are now Christians because God was a part of our every day play. God became real to them. He became even more real to us. The more He worked, the more we trusted Him to work. This gave us confidence to go SO MUCH MORE boldly to the throne to ask Him to work. Meanwhile, we played!

Our boys also knew that if they could not FIRST be nice to each other, they could not have friends over. They loved having friends over so they were pretty good with each other. Always? Oh no, but mostly. I know our boys are human. So am I. There were days I did not want others around. I wanted "just" an OB day. My favorite of all favorites was watching our boys play together and hearing their laughter. There still is nothing I love more. I understand why God feels that way too! Nothing makes Him smile more than seeing His children get along! In fact, God affirms that in Psalms 133:1, "How good and pleasant it is when brothers live together in unity!" (I throw in "sisters" for our granddaughters ;)

Believing it was my job to teach our boys to look for ways to make Jesus smile, I asked God for some creative ideas. God reminded me He really likes the whole idea of serving; in fact, says it was His idea! Cool, eh? In Deuteronomy 10:12, God tells us to, "SERVE the Lord your God with ALL your heart and with ALL your soul." Jesus even tells us in Matthew 20:26 & 28, "Whoever wants to be great among you must be your servant...the Son of Man did not come to be served, but to serve." Why do we think WE should be served? Ephesians 6:7 reminds us to "Serve wholeheartedly as if you were serving the Lord." Some of our favorite outings were to go serve "As unto the Lord." We liked going to the homes of older people and showing off Jesus, in word and deed, with various acts of kindness. We really loved going to the homes of widows and shoveling driveways or picking up pinecones from their yard. Okay, we did not ALWAYS love it, and sometimes wanted to be noticed and thanked. However, we remembered our purpose was to bring Jesus the glory and to see His smile. It was not for the attention or praise from others. He always sees what we do for others, and, if our heart is right, smiles.

When you have five sons, people remember...especially as they grew bigger and stronger! Neighbors would call and ask if any of the boys were home and, if so, would they come and help them move this or that. Families moving in the church would try to schedule their moves to coordinate when the boys were available. Two Men and a Truck started with the O'B boys + 3 + Dad who most often went along to oversee the move.

One time Michael was not at home to go out with the boys, much to my chagrin. As it was a Snow Day, Josh and Matt were home from school. A lady down the street called and asked if there was any way she could "borrow" our boys for a short time to help her boyfriend move. I knew this lady and thought it would be fine. THEN, the boyfriend came to pick up the boys. Remember, it was a Snow Day, so no school because the roads were not good. I had failed to ask enough questions. Not only did this boyfriend plan on taking our boys OUT of the neighborhood for this move, but he was really weird looking. Crazy eyes; kind of like one of those jiggly dolls you see up on the dashboard of some cars with the eyes bouncing all over – hard to talk to because you did not know where to look. Wanting to be a nice person (the boys would have questioned that!) I relinquished my protective hold on our boys and let them go with Crazy Eyes. As they left they were looking at me like, "MOMMMMMMMMMM!!!" He told me they would be back within the hour. One hour passed. Two hours passed. I called our neighbor. She assured me they would be back soon. Almost THREE hours later his truck pulled up in the driveway and the boys rushed into the house. Crazy Eyes came up on the porch and thanked me for letting him use their muscles. He said he would call again when he was ready for more help. I told him "No thank you, they would not be available." When I closed the door, Josh and Matt came out of hiding with stories of Crazy Eyes and his scary driving, pitiful language, and the "haunted house" they had gone to in downtown Lansing with a pit bull. I apologized again and again. I had to admit, now that they were home safely, their stories were pretty funny. They did not think so! Yes, serving is a good thing, but when in doubt, don't.

CAUTION: Usually when I do not want to serve it has nothing to do with any danger, except the danger of selfishness. Always ask God to let you see yourself as He sees you. Remember that serving does bring Him a smile. Specifically when I do not feel like serving, I go into it saying, "As unto you, Lord," and it is amazing how He changes my attitude. Sometimes people notice and He is glorified. But ALWAYS God sees it and is blessed. I like blessing God. I LOVE seeing His smile!

On April 8th in **God Calling**, it emphasizes the "marks of the Kingdom" and how "My children must be outstanding. I called a Peculiar People to make known My Name…willing to be deemed 'fools' for My Sake…known by the Marks that distinguish those of My Kingdom." No surprise, I have been called peculiar and foolish before…that is okay. Not just to be silly, but to be different, unique, to stand out for Jesus.

Sometimes I lose faith in people. We used to have a neighbor who was a friend, but a doubting friend. Always. We both would walk in our neighborhood, sometimes together. One morning she was walking with another friend and it was raining. As we passed each other she said, "Make it stop raining, Susie." I disgustedly smiled and negatively prayed, "Like that will make her believe, don't bother, Lord." Then I wondered. Should I have asked for her? Within seconds, the rain let up and stopped. I felt God saying to me, "Your job is to lift things up to me and Mine is to do what I choose – THEN you point them out." The next lap I chose to appear foolish and pointed out that the rain had stopped, pointing to the blue sky. Who knows? GOD KNOWS!!! GOD can take little or no faith from there – it is not my job to judge whether a "miracle" is deemed worthy.

On April 13th, God Calling continues saying, "Try to see the heart I see. Try, before you interview anyone, or speak to anyone, to ask ME to act as interpreter between you two." He knows the word, gesture, or touch that they need, or maybe it is just listening with your heart. On April 18 it says, "Love is God. Give them Love, and you give them God. Then leave Him to do His Work. Love all, even the beggars. Send no one away without a word of cheer, a feeling that you care." I believe God always wants us to leave people better than how they came to us, even if it is "just" a smile. When we allow God to fill us, interpret, and lead, HIS SPIRIT is free to help us show Him off!

Life can be great fun when we are open to being "peculiarly" foolish for Jesus. Sometimes people need to see a person not afraid to be different from those around them, to stand out in a crowd. NOT for attention sake, for Jesus' sake! Our son, Matt, and his roommate, Dave Nesbitt, are in their second year at U of M. God is growing them by leaps and bounds in their walk with Him and those He brings into their lives. They are working with Young Life at the high school level. Matt and Dave like to have fun, and they can act pretty goofy. They do not think they are above high schoolers, and because of that, the kids are drawn to them. Dave has a saying I really like, "Who's the noobe now?" Are you willing to be a noobe? Jesus might even laugh! After all, we know God has a sense of humor – just look at His animal kingdom, specifically us humans!

Other ways you can show off the Lord is through our daily conversations. How many times do you hear people say:

> **"Who knows?"**
> "What next is going to happen?"
> "Why do people get cancer?"
> "Why are there earthquakes, tornados, hurricanes, tsunamis?"
> "What will tomorrow bring?"
> **Simple answer: God knows!**

> Same with the question:
> **"Who cares?**
> "About what grade you get?"
> "About your job?"
> "What chair you are in band?"
> "Whom you marry?"
> **Same answer: God cares!**

If it points to God and His glory, I do not mind being dorky, do I boys?!! Instead of "luck" getting all of the credit, give credit to God. Acknowledge God's nature instead of Mother Nature. Show off God by drawing attention to Him.

A great song showing off our Lord is **"Top of My Lungs" by Craig & Dean Phillips.** Unashamedly, they sing about recognizing Who has saved us and wanting to proclaim it at the top of their lungs to all of the world. Ask God to help you show Him off. He is quite creative, you know! As I drive into the parking lot at work, I try to remember to ask God to help me show Him off. I want God's light in me to shine so that those around me will see the Father and be drawn to Him evermore…so **MUCH MORE!**

CHAPTER 17

CHOOSING LIFE

"For in Him we live and move and have our being."
Acts 17:28

God is my life. Does that sound too simple? Remember, I told you I am a simple person and handle life better when I think … simply. I once had a conversation with my favorite aunt and told her that God is my life. She told me that was silly. She said there was so much more to life than "just" God. I knew what she meant. Our lives are comprised of so many varying parts. Webster defines the word "whole" by saying that the "whole comprises the parts; the parts do not comprise the whole, nor is the whole comprised of its parts." God is my whole. I am a part. You are a part. Everything in our lives are parts. GOD IS LIFE. God is complete. I am complete in Him.

I have chosen God to be MY life. Indeed, this book is full of talk about choices. We start by believing God, choosing to remember Him and declare His praises, choosing to put on blinders to see Him more clearly, to hear Him more acutely, to abide with Him daily, to obey Him unreservedly, to follow Him more nearly, and to love Him more dearly. Choices direct my life. Whether people agree or not, I have chosen to look for Jesus' smile alone. It is in Him that I live, move, and have my being!

Rich Mullins says, "Stuff of life competes for the allegiance I owe only to You." It is so easy for me to get wrapped up in things of life that zap me of my energy for God, things I **choose** to allow in my life that misdirect His path for me. Spiritual blinders help me focus…NOT blind me from reality. Spiritual blinders do not let reality distract me from God! Remember, ultimately, GOD IS REALITY. But our life is quite real too. I want to live and move and have my whole being in Him.

MercyMe says in their song, **"All of Creation"** that the very reason we breathe is to sing of His glory. AMEN! I want my life to point to His life. My favorite gospel is John. The first chapter speaks of Jesus, the Word, becoming flesh and "In Him was life, and that life was the light of men" (John 1:4). It goes on to speak of Jesus' cousin, John the Baptist, "Sent from God… as a witness to testify concerning that light…he himself was not the light; he came ONLY as a witness to the light" (verses 7-8). What is really cool is we have the same purpose as John. We are sent from God to witness and testify concerning that Light; to point to the Light and share His life. Sometimes we forget that life is NOT all about us, that we are not THE light. John said he wanted to "Make straight the way for the Lord" (verse 23). John also loved pointing out Jesus, not wanting anyone to miss Him. John shouts out, "Look, the Lamb of God" (verses 29 and 36). One of my greatest goals in all of life is to make it easy for people to see Jesus, to prepare the way for God to step into their life by doing everything possible to make them hunger for Him. I never want to be an obstacle to turn them away from Jesus. I desire every breath to birth new life for His Kingdom. Big desire? Yes! BIGGER GOD!!! He wants that and **SO MUCH MORE** for us!

Birthdays have always been important to me. I like presents! More than that, I love to celebrate life! Michael and the boys (and now girls ;) have wonderfully obliged me, stretching my birth DAY to a birth WEEK and now I go for the whole MONTH! I figure after 50, why not?! I was born on July 17 so also instituted it into time – at 7:17 (am or pm) I say, "Happy Birthday to Me!" Self-centered? Yes. Sick? Maybe. Fun?

Absolutely!! Nothing wrong with celebrating life! Being stuck alone with me the longest when all his other brothers took off, our youngest son, Matt, became a pro at being aware of the time and wishing me a happy birthday. So many times we would be around other people and it would turn 7:17 and Matt would say, "Happy Birthday, Mom!" Those around would say, "I didn't know it was your birthday." Of course we would laugh and explain our goofiness.

God tells us in Deuteronomy 30:19-20 to "**CHOOSE LIFE** so that you and your children may live and that you may love the Lord your God, listen to His voice, and hold fast to Him. For **THE LORD IS YOUR LIFE**." Why do we find ourselves apologizing for making Him first? Why do we make excuses for NOT making Him first? If HE is our LIFE, what else matters? Climbing the corporate ladder? It is just a ladder. When we get to the top, we are just at the top. Why are we impressed by doctors, lawyers, and scientists who spend their lives studying life but ignore the Giver of Life? St. Augustine said, "Men go abroad to wonder at the heights of mountains, at the huge waves of the sea, at the long courses of the rivers, at the vast compass of the ocean, at the circular motions of the stars, and they pass by themselves without wondering." We pass by the Creator of all of these wonders. Why do we not wonder about THE Wonder? **There is SO MUCH MORE to life…JESUS**. When we follow Him, HE completes us. HE lives and moves and has HIS being in us.

It is hard to explain how God fills us, how He leads us. Last week Matt finished his second year of college. Michigan's economy is tough and summer jobs are few. In Danny's scheming to get us to all move down to Florida, he offered Matt a job working with him in commercial real estate. With mixed emotions and no alternative jobs, Michael and I surrendered what we thought would be "our" time with Matt for the summer. Michael and I drove with him and unloaded our 6' 4" baby where he would live with Danny, Kristin, and their three precious girls – I was jealous. In the midst of my jealously, I was also thrilled he would not only have time with them, but also with his brother, John, and his wife, Vanessa. They all attend and are actively involved in a wonderful church where Matt looked forward to connecting and working with the youth group. This is all good. The whole trip was marvelous with great conversation. Despite the rain for several hours, the weather inside the car had SONshine flowing freely. Special. Special in talk, special in quiet, special singing along to the music together. Matt is an incredible conversationalist, skillfully engaging his parental companions. He asked me about this book and how I knew what and when God wanted me to write. I told him I have learned over many years with God when it is me that wants to talk or God that wants me to talk... and what He wants me to say. "How?" he asked. I told him I always get a burning sensation, an impelling urge. Without missing a beat, Matt said, "Oh, that is God speaking? I just thought I was ADD. So next time I get a fever and can't sit still, I will know I am suppose to write!" Smart Alec! So much like ... his father!!!

This chapter on choosing life would not be complete without me mentioning that I am PRO LIFE. I also am pro-choice in the sense I believe we all have a choice to have guarded or unguarded sex before, during, and after marriage. Of course, the ONLY guarantee we have to not get pregnant is NO sex. I also believe that we are responsible for our choices and the consequences of those choices. If I get pregnant in the middle of my choice, I will deal with the consequences of my choice, despite convenience, affordability, or timing. The innocent life conceived in the pregnancy has no choice. Yet daily we allow our nation to partake in the greatest of all holocausts, abortion. We will fight and makes laws protecting "endangered species" like owls, whales, plants, and even snails, yet kill off our very own. God forgive us!

Being raised in a politically acute family with my Dad in politics early on to my brother involved in various offices, I grew to love my country and its' branches of government. My parents were Democrats for years and years. Then as the tide changed, my Dad saw the more conservative values of the

Republican Party and probably voted more Republican in his latter years. My brother, being a student of history and government, is an amazing bipartisan and can unite both sides. He runs on the Democratic ticket. I am a one issue American – PROLIFE. I vote for the candidate who is FOR life, despite the other issues, and have been accused of being a simple, small minded Christian. What is more important than life? Education? Finances? Healthcare? War? Peace? The mindset of life affects the outcome of each of these. If a person is not FOR life, I do not care where they stand on other issues.

One of my very favorite things in all of life is worshipping with our children. As we were flying home early Monday morning, we were able to go with the kids on Sunday to their church. We were blessed with great music and teaching. A bonus was their call to worship, explaining beautifully why we are here, why we are alive! I have printed it off to carry with me. I want to use it as a check list on prioritizing, to remind me always that JESUS is my life, NOT all the noisy busy-ness that pulls me in sixteen different directions.

God Calling on May 9 &10, shares how a calm life, not a hurried-scurried life, unfolds harmony within oneself. "It is your task to maintain your own heart peace in adverse circumstances. Harmony is always yours when you strain your ear to catch Heaven's music. All agitation is destructive of good. All calm is constructive of good, and at the same time destructive of evil. When man wants evil destroyed so often he rushes to action. It is wrong. First BE STILL and KNOW that I AM GOD. Then act only as I tell you. Always calm with God. Calm is trust in action. Only trust, perfect trust, can keep one calm." Isaiah 30:15 says, "In quietness and in confidence shall be your strength." I have paraphrased Isaiah 26:3 to say, "God will keep me in perfect peace if I keep my mind on Him."

Truly it is "in Him we live and move and have our being." **CHOOSING LIFE GOD'S WAY** frees us to be **God's MUCH MORE!!!**

WE ARE HERE
by Igniter Media

We are not here out of obligation, or tradition, or fear, or guilt
We are not here just to sing, preach, be entertained
We are not here to rewrite what He has written
We are not here to alter what He has spoken
We are not here to shout over what He whispers
Rather, we are here to ECHO HIS GLORY
Not trumpet ours
We are here to celebrate the love that was proved on
the cross
We are here to magnify His name so that others might
come
We are here because God loved us first
We are here because He has called us into
community
We are here because the Gospel is the GOOD NEWS
And IT has forever changed us
We are here to worship
To worship our Creator
To worship our Father
To worship our Redeemer,
To worship our Savior
We are here to receive His grace and mercy
To offer our bodies as living sacrifices
To surrender ourselves to His Will
We are here to echo Him
ECHO HIM with our lives, our passions, all we have
That is why we sing
That is why we celebrate
That is why we are here

Used with permission
Text from the video "We Are Here" by Igniter Media
(IgniterMedia.com)

CHAPTER 18

HIDE AND SEEK

"Since, then, you have been raised with Christ,
set your hearts on things above,
where Christ is seated at the right hand of God.
Set your minds on things above, not on earthly things.
For you died, and
YOUR LIFE IS NOW HIDDEN WITH CHRIST IN GOD.
When Christ, Who IS YOUR LIFE appears,
Then you also will appear with Him in glory."
Colossians 3:1-4

We have all played the game of Hide and Seek sometime in our lifetime. I never liked it. I hate being chased or hunted down. As a child, I would step out to show my hiding place before I was found because otherwise I would scream and I hate screaming even more. Makes me feel like a baby… instead, I am clearly a Scaredy Cat.

Once when I was about 9, I felt totally ignored by everyone. It was a beautiful summer day and I wanted to play outside but could not get anyone to play with me. I even went to my Mom. She was busy taking care of us, wanting things done before my Dad got home from work. I told her I was going to go eat worms. She laughed, knowing better. I told her I was going to run away. Again, she knew better. So I decided to show her!

I went and crawled under my Mom and Dad's bed and laid really, really still for HOURS!!!! (okay, maybe 68 minutes). No one came to look for me. No one even missed me!!! I crawled out and went up to my Mom and said, "I'm back!"

She said, "Good." I went outside and played...playing is much more fun than hiding!

When our sons, Steve and Josh were little, they made up a game called Runaway Kids. We moved to Mt. Pleasant in 1988 and Johnny and Danny started school in the fall. With their instigators gone for the day, Stevie Deevie stepped into the leadership role and Joshie Woshie (Yes, those were my very clever nicknames for them that helped to make them MEN today!) willingly followed. They were the best of buddies and could play for hours and hours. I would have to go check on them because they could hide away in their "man cave" forever playing with Lincoln Logs, Legos, and Transformers. We had a very functional house that was perfect for us in the greatest of neighborhoods. It was an 1800 square foot ranch with a full basement so LOTS of room to run and hide. The boys' favorite place to play was on this open 4' X 8' X 4' lofty shelf thingee built to the left as you go down to the basement for storage. I know this because it was high enough for me to sit straight up and read them stories, wide enough they could move around without falling and long enough they could stretch out for their naps...which they sometimes did. They could not have been much more than 3 and 5 when they started playing this game. They would see their brothers off to school and then run to get all of their equipment needed for a lifetime...or at least until lunch ;) My Dad had found these adorable little dorky plastic backpacks at a garage sale which they would load up. Stevie would usually grab some sort of hat, as would his shadow. Joshie must have thought he was David ready to slay giants because he usually had rocks and some snack in case they got delayed getting "home" (even tho' they were just steps from the kitchen ;) Josh would grab books, Steve would grab guns. Sometimes they would add jackets and boots to their attire, always wanting to be prepared...you never know when the next storm will be hitting the basement! They played this game for years. We would often eat a snack there, sometimes our lunch. It was always adorably amusing to see how they would prepare for each day. As they grew, so did their range of hideouts! In nice weather, outside, under bushes, out in the garage...sometimes in our van... remember the Chick Mobile? Even when we moved in 1993 and they both were in school themselves, they would return to their fantasy world after school, on Saturdays, and during summer vacation. Matt was born in 1990. Once he was big enough, they would sometimes let him join their outing, now in a new territory but always their domain. Matt became the shadow, Josh gained prestige, and Steve remained in charge.

Runaway Kids was a delight to Steve and Josh. I think of how I like to runaway, need to runaway, at times myself. Sometimes I need to escape the commotion of life, always to run to God, and hide in Christ. This usually does not incorporate a physical running away...and never without my family – they are my haven here on earth. It does often embody a "distancing" from the world around me by turning off the phone, staying away from internet, or going for a walk. Many cannot believe I will ignore the phone and are offended...sorry, too bad. I do not aim to offend. I do aim to recharge, emptying myself of this world, filling myself with God. To do so for me, I find myself needing to Hide and Seek...to be a God Seeker!

God tells us to seek Him. He also tells us that when we seek Him, we will find Him. I love how Jesus tells us He longs for us too. In Matthew 23:37, Jesus says, "How often I have longed to gather your children together, as a hen gathers her chicks under her wings, but you were not willing." I think of the freedom of my kids to run away and hide, feeling safe, secure. Too often I believe our world tells us as adults we need to stand strong, hold your ground, advance, attack; when all we want to do, all we need to do, is run into the loving arms of Jesus! God wraps me in His love in Psalms 57:1–3, "Have mercy on me, O God, have mercy on me, for in You my soul takes refuge. I **will** take refuge in the shadow of Your wings, until the disaster has passed. I cry out to God Most High, to God who fulfills His purpose for me. He sends from Heaven and saves me, rebuking those who hotly pursue me; God sends His love and His faithfulness." It is a choice to seek refuge in the arms of God.

I am restored when I hide away in Him and remember my Refuge, He Who holds me securely in the shadow of His wings. When my soul is parched, I run to Him. Psalms 143: 5-6 says, "I remember the days of long ago; I meditate on all Your works and consider what Your hands have done. I spread out my hands to You; my soul thirsts for You like a parched land." God delights in restoring our parched soul, in bringing refreshment to our lives through His Spirit.

Too many times I have hidden from those around me what I truly believe God wants me to partake in, with or without those around me. Balance can be difficult to discern. As a conservative Christian, sometimes I am fearful I will offend others. I can become more concerned with that, than whether I will offend God if I do not act on His Spirit's prodding. I am specifically talking about how I struggle with my personal positioning during corporate worship – whether I sit, stand, kneel, or raise my hands. It is neither right nor wrong to do any of these in worship, unless God directs you. It took me years to step out, to put blinders on so that I could look at God's face and not all of those around me. I came to realize I needed to stand, kneel, or raise my hands when I felt God wanted me to surrender to Him, to adore Him, to point to Him, to honor Him. I would pray, "Lord, what if this offends someone?" I felt Him saying, "Susan, what if you offend **Me** if you do not do what I say? I want you abandoned to Me. Sold out!" Depending on the crowd, I still struggle. Then I read this scripture in Exodus 9:29, "I spread out my hands to You." I see it as an outward acknowledgment that I need His help. Sometimes it is a surrender of my will to His will, like "SURRENDER, HANDS UP!" Many times it is simply pointing to Jesus, recognizing everything is all about Him, NOT me.

Our little Madeline, who was two at the time, had a favorite song and would always shout it out when we were asking what song to sing next. It took a little help from her interpreter, Sydney, to let us know she was saying, "I Stand." The song is very much about God's power in creation and His deep love for us that took our sins to the cross, freeing us to live for Him, in awe, to be abandoned to Him. The real name is **"The Stand" by Hillsong United** but I love that even at two, Madeline, instinctively knew she needed to personalize it and would stand in her Daddy's arms with her little hands lifted up and eyes closed. Did she know what she was doing? Probably not, but she was copying what had been modeled to her by her parents.

MUCH of what we learn is caught more than taught. Just as Matt shadowed the Runaway Kids and Madeline is learning how to worship God from her parents, I want to imitate Jesus by seeking His Father, running to Him, hiding in Christ. As Colossians 3:3 says, I want to "Be hidden with Christ in God." Shielded. Nurtured. I want to be surrounded by His love, filled with His Spirit. Psalms 46:1 tell us, "God is our **REFUGE** and strength, an ever-present help in trouble."

God makes this and **SO MUCH MORE** available to us. How **MUCH MORE** could I want? How **MUCH MORE** could you want?

143

CHAPTER 19

BACK AWAY

*"But **YOU**, Man of God, **Flee** from all of this,*
*and **pursue righteousness**."*
I Timothy 6:11

As a daily reminder, our son, Danny, has his daughters, Sydney (5) and Madeline (3) yell out to him as he leaves for work, "But YOU, Man of God, flee from all of this, and pursue righteousness!" I am sure it will not be long before Elisabeth (1 ½) joins them in this standard practice, much more for Dan's sake than for theirs. How wonderful to include your family in your daily quest, bringing to the forefront of your mind our need to flee temptation and pursue His ways!

Becoming a strong Christian is not standard. Sadly, the majority of Christians today have accepted Jesus as their Savior, but leave Him on the cross. Will they still get into Heaven when they die? Guess that is up to the Savior. I always wonder why people want to go to Heaven if they do not even want to spend any time with Jesus now. Will they recognize Him at the gate? How will they know His voice? It is very scary to think He may plainly say, "I never knew you." Jesus warns us of this in Matthew 7:23. Then what?!!! If Jesus is what we long for in Heaven and we receive Christ at salvation, then

Heaven starts NOW at your salvation. Why are we not living like Heaven is now? It is because we do not know Him.

There are many good people who flee evil, but never pursue Jesus. Likewise, there are many who pursue Jesus, but never flee evil. The two cannot mix. Pastor Brown of the Kalamazoo Gospel Mission said he was saved at the age of 13 but started "living saved" later. What does that mean? It means at 13 he received a Savior but surrendered to His Lordship when he started "living saved." DO NOT SETTLE for salvation when God intends you to have Heaven here on earth through the Lordship of Christ. Please hear my heart. Earth is NOT Heaven. Heaven is life with Christ. God intends us to have SO MUCH MORE by fleeing evil and pursuing righteousness!

When I was learning to drive, my parents would wisely counsel me, "When in doubt, don't." That applied when turning in front of a vehicle – if we were not sure if there was enough time to clear, do not turn. If road conditions were not good and I doubted the safety of driving the posted speed limit, don't...go at a safe speed. I learned to take that application into all of my life...when in doubt, don't. I used it in high school when I was dating a guy two years older than me and he wanted to go to a party I knew my parents would not approve of. I asked him to take me home. I clung to it in college when friends invited me to do things I did not feel comfortable doing. I asked God to give me a sensitive spirit to His Spirit. I asked Him to help me feel His nudge to stop. My Mom prayed for me to have that sensitive, responsive spirit to God. God always answers when His Will is prayed. He wants us to flee evil and pursue Him.

Two great books that come from different angles on this are **The Pursuit of Holiness by Jerry Bridges** and **Don't Waste Your Life by John Piper**. John says that much of our struggles exist when we start calling earth home. He says,

"I start to fit in. I start to love what others love...before I know it, I am calling luxuries "needs" and using my money just the way unbelievers do. I begin to forget the war. I don't think much about people perishing. Missions and unreached peoples drop out of my mind. I stop dreaming about the triumphs of grace. I sink into a secular mindset that looks first to what man can do, not what God can do. It is a terrible sickness. And I thank God for those who have forced me again and again toward a wartime mind-set" (page 112).

If our single, all-embracing passion is to make much of Christ in life and death, and if the life that magnifies Him most is the life of costly love, then life is risk, and risk is right. To run from it is to waste your life" (page 79).

Satan knows us; not like God knows us through and through, but Satan knows our weaknesses. With or without Jesus, Satan knows if we have any morals at all, we will not be drawn away by obvious evils. He is much more subtle than that. He will try to lure us away from God's best by offering good things to do. Nothing wrong with good things, but are they best? We have just so much time in the day and a measured amount of energy to do them…even with caffeine. John Piper says Christians often try to fit in and walk as close to the edge of Satan's woo's as possible, never accounting for a gust of wind or a friendly push. We think we are infallible. The greatest sin of all is pride…making ourselves god. The reason we need a Savior is simply that we NEED a Savior! Some say living like Jesus is impossible. **Kutless**, in their song, **"What Faith Can Do,"** says that we use the word impossible just to excuse not trying. Jesus tells us with Him, all things are possible - specifically being Christ-like. When Satan lures you with his attractions, **BACK AWAY** from the edge. Once you step over the line you start falling at a faster and faster pace on a downward spiral. **FLEE!!! DON'T SETTLE** for anything but GOD's best…His **MUCH MORE**.

BEWARE: I am going to be stepping on toes…again. My Mom's Dad, Grandpa Johnson, was an alcoholic. In his later years, he gave up drinking and eventually became a Christian. I credit much of that to my parent's loving, consistent care of him and my Grandma. He even lived with my parents his final year of life. Because of my Grandpa's drinking, my Mom never drank, she hated it.

With her as my model, my mentor, I never drank either and came to hate it too. I saw the destructive nature of drinking when I was in college. MUCH MORE than that, I learned that scientifically our reasoning is formatted in the frontal lobe of the brain. As a Minister, Michael went to a seminar on Alcohol and Chemical Dependency at Brighton Hospital. Medical doctors taught that alcohol and drugs first attack the frontal lobe of our brain, dulling our reasoning power. God works through that which He has created. Therefore, it is reasonable to ascertain that it is through the frontal lobe the Holy Spirit works to convict us, to "nudge" us. The decision not to drink was sealed for me that day. I never wanted to dull the Spirit's working in my life. I forever yearned to be sensitive and responsive to His leading, guiding, nudging, protecting, and loving. Not unaware of Satan's other tactics to distract me from God's best, I try to carry that over into every area of my life. I purpose to not be dulled to His Spirit by lack of sleep or exercise, too much food, medication that controls me instead of me controlling it, addictive work, consuming people, or a life void of His Daily Bread. My husband's brother, Jerry, was killed at 37 when he left the bar and crossed over the center line. He left behind two sons, Jay (7) and Steven (4) whose lives had already been damaged by divorce due to Jerry's alcoholism. Even in my own family this issue of drinking is contested. They say all in moderation. I do NOT want to be moderate when it comes to God. I cannot control others, but I can choose to control myself...to flee evil and pursue righteousness.

We do not go to R-rated movies. Given, many PG-13 are just as bad, as are an excess of the commercials on television. I cannot control Hollywood or the news media. I can control what I allow to come into my brain and what I dwell on. James Allen says, "You are today where your thoughts have brought you; you will be tomorrow where your thoughts take you." We choose. God tells us in II Corinthians 10:5 to "Take captive every thought to make it obedient to Christ." In that, we have victory!

In his book, <u>The Pursuit of Holiness</u>, Jerry Bridges says, "Pursue holiness, for without holiness no one will see the Lord (Hebrews 12:14)...the word pursue suggests two thoughts: first, that diligence and effort are required; and second, that it is a lifelong task...holiness is a process" (page 11). I am FAR from being holy, but I want to be diligent to put forth whatever effort necessary to see the Lord! Strangely, it is comforting to me to know it is a lifelong process and does not happen overnight. I have been at this since I first met Jesus at 5 years old. Jerry continues with "Christians fail to understand their own responsibility for holiness. If we sin, it is because we choose to sin – not because we lack the ability to say no to temptation. We are not defeated; we are simply disobedient" (chapter 8). Ouch! The truth hurts. Instead we need to **BACK AWAY!!! FLEE!!! DON'T SETTLE** for the world's standards!!! **PURSUE RIGHTEOUSNESS!!!** Psalms 101:2-3 says, "I will walk in my house with a blameless heart. I will set before my eyes no vile thing." It is a choice.

Satan attacks marriages and family. He is quite aware that they are something sacred to God. We need to do all we can to avoid any temptation, recognizing many temptations are thrown our way daily. A simple deterrent is to wear your wedding band. Sounds silly, I know, but I am amazed at how many men do not wear their wedding ring. Most women have dreamed about getting married so they love to wear their ring. I have even scolded a few brothers, explaining my reasoning. I believe most people on the prowl will not purpose to go after married people. So if you can block even one affront by simply wearing your ring, do it! I have had men and women tell me they cannot wear their ring at work because it is too dangerous...then put it on after work.

I am sad to say I had a personal experience with this. When I was in college and working during the summer, I met a nice guy who was a very kind Social Worker in the Juvenile Division where I was working. We played softball on the same team and I came to know him, so I thought, quite well. One night after a game he asked me if I wanted to go grab a bite to eat. I said sure! Afterwards, he invited me back to his house to visit a little more and I naively, or stupidly, said yes. When we arrived at his house, I wandered around looking at his pictures. In several there was a beautiful woman with him. I asked him who she was. He said his wife. His wife??!! WHAT?!!! He said not to be alarmed, that it was okay that we were out because they were currently separated!!! I said it was NOT okay to be out and asked him to take me back to my car so I could go home. IF I had seen a wedding band, NO WAY would I have ever gone out to eat nor returned to his house with him. I purpose to avoid every temptation of evil – adultery is evil! Adultery is sin. Do we call sin, SIN? God does.

With my eyes being opened, I became more sensitive to married men having lunch with other women, married and single, and vice versa. I know this is not a common way of thinking but being Christ-like is not common. Many would say there is no harm in sharing a meal with the opposite sex who is not your mate. I disagree. I see red flags go up and cry out DANGER!!! **FLEE!!!** DON'T SETTLE for doing things the way of the world. When we were in campus ministry, many times girls would ask Michael to join them for different things. I see it differently when a bunch of guys are with a bunch of gals. One girl asked Michael if he would go to a play with her. Imagine this…he asked me! I bet you know my answer! The same girl had the nerve to ask him to play paddle ball with her…same answer!!! Prudish? Maybe…but also avoiding temptation.

Temptation will happen, but we do not have to bring it on ourselves. Jesus tells us to be "Shrewd as snakes, and as innocent as doves" (Matthew 10:16). Satan is on the prowl. I Peter 5: 8-9 says we must "Be self-controlled and alert. Your enemy, the devil, prowls around like a roaring lion looking for someone to devour. Resist him, standing firm in the faith." He is out to swallow you whole! **FLEE!**

Michael and I are careful not to get emotionally involved with anyone but each other. That is not to say we do not have friends of the opposite sex. However, we do not spend any length of time on the phone, internet, or in person, one on one with another of the opposite sex. Women should counsel women, men should counsel men. Of course, Michael, in the ministry, often meets with various women but always has his door open with his secretary right across the hall. For extensive counseling, he refers women to other women. We also avoid riding alone with the opposite sex or having them come to the house if our spouse is not at home. Not wanting anyone to ever question what we may be doing, we try to "avoid all appearances of evil" (I Thessalonians 5:22, KJV). We make enough mistakes in our lives – we do not want to make someone else stumble by sloppy choices we make. Heaven forbid that anyone ever say, "Well, Susie O'Berski does it so I can do it." We are all tempted in different ways. What does not tempt me, may tempt you and vice versa. As sisters and brothers in Christ, we want to guard one another. I find it even helpful to think on other men as brothers or fathers in the faith. It is amazing how you start thinking differently toward someone when you realize they are family! I also choose to dress modestly so as not to draw a man's eyes toward my body. Sometimes I will even ask Michael if a shirt is too clingy or pants too tight. I want to attract people to Jesus, not me. As mother of five sons and a wife of one husband, I plead with you women to dress yourselves and your daughters appropriately with a desire to guard your brothers.

I want my life to SHOUT OUT clearly to the world around me that I belong to JESUS!!! I am wonderfully reminded in the song by **Casting Crowns, "Lifesong,"** that there is no sacrifice too small for my Lord. I, too, want my life song to sing for Jesus! DAILY, I want my life to delight Him, to bring Him a smile. What attraction of this world could bring me more joy than His smile?!!!

God has **SO MUCH MORE** for us once we start taking Him seriously. **BACK AWAY** from and **DON'T SETTLE** for the lures of this world. **Be God's MUCH MORE by fleeing evil and pursuing His righteousness! CHOOSE TO BE GOD'S MUCH MORE!!!**

CHAPTER 20

SHADOWS

*"Even though I walk through the valley of
the shadow of death,
I will fear no evil, for YOU are with me."*
Psalms 23:4

S hadows are not real. We cannot touch them, hear them, smell them, or taste them. BUT, we can see them – they are bigger than life! I so remember when each one of our boys saw their own shadow for the first time and the delight it was to try to catch it, jump on it, and run from it. It was also great fun to attempt grabbing a brother's shadow or swallowing it up with their own shadow. Like Peter Pan's shadow that came off and Wendy had to sew it back on, shadows become elusive when we turn and face the sun. More than that, they disappear.

There are things in life that seem bigger than life and feel very real. Heartache. Confusion. Doubt. What does God mean when He talks about walking through the valley of the SHADOW of death? Is death not real? For sure, there is the sting of death (I Corinthians 15:55-56) when someone you love dies. Horrible shadows of fear can swallow us up in the great darkness that hovers over the loss. Yet, death is actually the reality of stepping into the Kingdom of Light and the eternal arms of God. Dr. Tom Malone, my minister growing up, used to say that for a Christian, death is a servant to usher us into the arms of the living God. Someone else told me that death is the key to unlock the door to eternity with Jesus! Both analogies make death sound a whole lot better. Of course, we can only enter through the blood of Jesus. Thankfully, Jesus made a way when He died on the cross and arose from the grave. I love that there was a curtain of separation between the Holy Place and Holy of Holies that was torn from top to bottom the moment Jesus died. Matthew 27:50-51 says, "When Jesus cried out again in a loud voice, He gave up His spirit. At that moment the curtain of the temple was torn in two from top to bottom." Ephesians 2:13-14 says, "Now in Christ Jesus you who once were far away have been brought near through the blood of Christ. For He Himself is our peace, Who has made the two (Jews and Gentiles) one (in Christ) and has destroyed the barrier, the dividing wall (curtain) of hostility." We need no high priest to intercede on our behalf; we have JESUS, THE High Priest.

Hillsong United sings a beautiful song, "**At the Cross**," that speaks of God's great love for us through Jesus. His act of sacrificial love upon the cross, shedding His blood for our sins tore the veil between us to make a way into His holy presence. No more shadows, no more veils – we stand face to face in His love.

Maybe shadows and death and pain are not about reality as much as they are about focus. God gave me a very simple analogy about shadows. It was during the time we were getting ready to move from my favorite friends, neighborhood and church in Brighton farrrrrrrrrr away (two hours north) to Mt. Pleasant. I remember having this one of several moaner/groaner conversations with God. Finally, I stopped long enough to listen. He reminded me that I had told Him He was in charge of my life and that I wanted Him to use me however and wherever HE thought best. I nodded in agreement that, sure enough, that had been the plan. With a little sarcasm, God even pointed out He could have sent me to

Siberia but was allowing me to stay in the same state, with the same language and comparable living conditions. What came next is something that has been bigger than life to me! **God told me I had been so busy looking at the shadows that I had forgotten to look at Him**. He then listed off every negative thought I had told Him. Yes, God has a pretty good memory, but He also had heard my complaints way too many times and was ready to bury them – so was I. This is when He reminded me shadows are not real, they occur when there is inadequate lighting. Shadows occur when an object (ie: fear, guilt, anger, distrust, shame, unforgiveness, or even a hurt) is blocking the light. Shadows disappear once you turn from the object causing the shadow and face the sun – THE SON! Instead of choosing to focus on all the so-called negatives in my life, I needed to turn my focus to God, and allow His Light to reveal His blessings.

TRY IT! Turn your back on whatever is darkening your path right now and look to Jesus! 180 degree turn – nothing part way. Look at Psalms 23:4 again, "Even though I walk through the valley of the SHADOW of death, I will fear no evil, for YOU are with me." David's focus was on God, not the shadows. Shadows fade in the Light of Jesus.

As you walk in God's light, **seeking HIS face and HIS smile,** He wants you to grasp this and **SO MUCH MORE!!!**

CHAPTER 21

SEASONS OF LIFE

"There is a time for everything,
and a season for every activity under heaven."
Ecclesiastes 3:1

A re you trying to fit too much into every day? Ponder this quote by George MacDonald, "I find the doing of the will of God leaves me no time for disputing about His plans." Everyone has 24 hours to each day. Gary Hawes, Founder and Executive Director of Michigan Christian Campus Ministries (commonly known as His House) says, "There is always enough time to do the perfect will of God." And Gary does. How? He stays on task. The mission of MCCM is to reach, teach, and send students out for Christ. Gary, the Board of Directors, and Staff are devoted to reaching and growing college students for the Kingdom. They recognize there are many good things they could be doing, but have chosen to stick to "the" plan and not let anything dilute or distract them from their calling from God.

We, too, need to stick to the plan and stay on task. Maybe we first need to figure out the plan. Maybe we need to recognize "this" is a season of our life and accept the plan. Besides God, there are few things that ever stay the same. The scripture, "It came to pass," is often comforting to me and a great reminder that whatever I am going through at the time is not "here" to stay. Funny how we never cling to that passage in the midst of things we enjoy. We do not want them to pass…yet there is a time for everything, and a season for every activity.

Far better is for us to look to God daily and trust Him in each season. More than that, to choose to thrive in each season! There is a great freedom when we recognize God's purpose for us in each day. God never intends us to do everything, nor does He want us to even attempt it. We are given 24 hours in each day to free us, not to limit us.

Sadly, there will always be people who never appreciate anything. We cannot do anything about that but love and pray for them. Just do not let it be YOU! There are those who want to be older, younger, in college, out of college, in a job, out of a job, home with the children, children out of the home, less busy, more busy, retired, needed, and a countless number of other wants.

Thankfully I had very wise parents who showed and reminded me to enjoy the moment, my current season in life. My Dad would say, "Carpe Diem!" Seize the day! God says the same thing in Colossians 4:5, "Make the most of every opportunity." Both see everything as opportunities. It is up to US to make the most of them! In the midst of five little boys it was sometimes hard to breathe, let alone enjoy the moment. Not really. It comes down to being a choice and a redirecting of our <u>focus</u>. Tired of that word yet? Hopefully not, as it **IS** a critical key to living an abundant life! Eyes on Jesus? JOY! Eyes on me and all my selfish woes? Misery! You <u>choose</u>! How 'bout that word? Read on!

People often ask me what age I enjoyed the most with our children. I tell them whatever age they are in! Seriously! I believe MUCH of what we get from our children is what we expect from them. I never called it "the terrible twos" but "the terrific twos." I looked forward to the teen years! I have thoroughly enjoyed each age…okay, that is a little bit of an exaggeration. I LOVED them through it, but I have to admit the odd years were the hardest with each son – isn't that crazy?!!!

Specifically 5, 7, 9, 11, and 13. Why? I do not know, but those did seem to be the years our boys were the most difficult with testing, tears and whining, which we did not allow. Somehow, even with our miracle children, the whining still got in there. I never minded the REAL tears due to falls from trees, crashes on bikes, baseballs in the eyes, heads colliding with bats, faces smashing into walls, fish hooks attacking the lip, wrought iron railing out to make an impression, back packs packed with a metal lunch box smacking into an ear, slips from the highest point of the jungle gym, or Superman (Steve at age 2) jet pro-pelled from top bunk bed by older brother (age concealed to protect the guilty, but Danny, you know who you are ;) into the marble sill only to find he could NOT fly! Heartbreak came with those tears, seeing my little guys hurting. It was when my little guys were hurting one another that got to me! Bottom line to all of this is that, most of the time, Michael and I chose to rec-ognize our boys were children and to enjoy them.

That season of our life was probably the one filled most with dirt...dirt in the house, out OF the sandbox, in most pockets, and filling every sock. It is that dirt, our 5 second rule, and **GOD** that probably kept us the healthiest, immu-nizing us from all of the germs of the day! Who says boys don't bring their own benefit plan?!!! No illness wants to attack a family that has shared every germ by eating out of the same ice cream carton during an ICE CREAM PARTY. Salmonella slithers away from the family that eats cookie dough and cake batter with uncooked eggs – oh no! Who wants cookie dough or batter with cooked eggs?!!! YUK!

Okay, I know you are all jealous here that YOU did not get the O'Berski boys. Even tho' jealousy is not a good thing, I do not blame you one bit... but too bad. Just more proof that God does have favorites! Ok, for those who do not know me, I am teasing you...sort of. But my dear hubby, whom I would not characterize as a mercy, is concerned you think I am prideful here and too cocky. I am cocky, (I prefer to call it confident ;) I think I am a Mom who is proud of her boys, not prideful. I see it differently. Pride says, "Look at what I have done." Being proud is recognizing something God has done and giving Him the credit with thanksgiving! I truly believe God, in His great wisdom, has chosen the best parent for each child and vice versa. So we should all think our kids are best! Our boys are a marvelous gift from God and we treasure them!

I also know we are talking about a "season" of life, but God has surrounded me with a "gender" for life – male. I thank Him! It boggles my mind that so many people have asked me if I was disappointed that I did not "get" a girl. Heavens to Betsy NO! Would we have been happy with a girl? By all means... but when you hold out your empty hands and ask God for His plans and He fills them with wonderful boys, you choose to PRAISE HIM and TRUST HIM! You choose to focus on His face and see Him smile as His plan unfolds and His creation explodes! BOYS!

As the boys grew in number and age, I realized I could not be as involved in Campus Ministry as I had been when I was single, newly married, or a mother of one or even two. God gives you two hands for a reason. When child #3 comes along with #1 and #2 louder and faster, something has to go so that you can focus in on caring best for the children. I had always wanted children, but when it started to "limit" my involvement in ministry, I struggled. My very wise Mom told me I needed to appreciate this season of my life, recognizing it passes way too quickly, and that there would be plenty of time later for leading Bible Studies and discipling students. Again she was right. Her wisdom also freed me to enjoy my children instead of seeing them as an interruption.

That does not mean I stopped being involved with ministry. Ministry is people caring for people. Michael and I wanted our boys to grow up caring for people, so that caring became as natural as breathing. So even tho' I would not always go to every meeting, I had the boys in and around the college students. They loved it and the students loved them. Many of our favorite students offered to babysit and we were thrilled to take them up on it. Sometimes they offered that service for free and sometimes we paid them because they needed the money. We wanted great people around our boys, AND we needed time to focus just on us. Almost every week the boys and I would make some kind of cake or cookies to take in for the weekly meeting. We usually would go in early to visit and stay at least for the music because the boys did not have to be so quiet. Our boys loved to go in and play with the students living in the Guy's House on campus, especially at University of Michigan and Central Michigan University. We loved that our guys could "hang out" with Godly college students and purposed to surround them with the best examples possible. At times, they also saw poor examples of godliness and how we loved and tried to care for those students anyway. I cannot count how many times we would get a phone call from someone with a desperate plea - I would grab whatever boys were around at the time and we would pray. Real life lessons from a precious season of life.

For good or for bad, ministry happens wherever people are. Our goal was always to touch people for good, **for God**. God provided me the freedom to not have to work outside the home. We wanted to take advantage of that not only on the campus, but in the neighborhoods where we lived, the churches to which we belonged, and with the families from which we came. When the boys were not in school, we had a lot more freedom to travel and visit with family because we did not have to worry about school. A great season! But I cannot say we really worried a whole lot about it anyway. Thankfully, our boys were good students. When I would want to go visit family or join Michael on an "outing," I would go in and talk with the teachers, asking for work our boys could do while gone so they would not get behind. Notice, I did not ask if we could take the boys. They were our children. God had put us in charge of them. I did pray before going in and always tried to establish good relations with all of our boys' teachers, along with their principals. Some I came to know a WHOLE lot better than others, right Danny? Joshie? ☺ Anyway, some teachers were not thrilled with us taking them and thought they would be missing too much. Nope, wrong! Family time is ALWAYS more important than any thing they might learn in school. My retired teacher/principal sister Kaye cringes when I say this but she lives in Connecticut so…oh well! Plus, I was a little afraid of her, so I did not always tell her.

School does add to life, as does sports. With five sons, we had to consciously choose to limit how many sports and activities they could be involved in each sporting season. Much against the public "warfare" of starting your kids out early so they get in the system and are the best at what they do, we wanted time together, not apart. Indeed, we wanted THE best for our boys and it was NOT to develop egomaniacs. We did not even let our sons begin a sport before they were eight years old – oh no! Believe me, it did not ruin them and "the system" became quite aware of them. Once John, Danny, and Steve were each in a sport it became crazy with practices and games. I truly had to adjust to not having dinners together every night as a family – I did not like that. However, God pointed out to me that it was another "season" in our life and to enjoy the time in the car to and from games and practices. The one on one time often allowed a captive audience.

We did sports as a family. We would go cheer for whoever was playing. Poor Matt ended up with the least amount of family fans because by the time he was in middle school, his older brothers were already away from home. Each, however, made attempts to return from college or their jobs to cheer for him as he had cheered for them. Michael was incredible in being there for our boys. He always made it very clear wherever he was working what his priorities were – first God, second family, so at best, job (even tho' ministry) was third. It was hard for them to argue because God affirms that order. Plus, Michael always put in more than enough time and would often get more done in one day than many others would in a week. Yes, I am partial to him too!

Graduation from high school was another "season" of life for us. I noticed the void probably more so than Michael because I was at home with the boys. It was not so bad with John because, bless his little heart, he chose to stay local for the first two years and live at home. So in many ways, it was better because there were times he would be home when the other guys were at school so I had even more time with him. John was an awesome help with running his brothers to work or practice and joining us at games when he did not have classes or work. The transition went smoothly. Then the "smoothness" started breaking down!

Danny graduated the next year in 1999 and moved to Ann Arbor, studying at UM. One of the MANY super things about having a large family is that there is always someone around. So I was okay…even though Danny was missed lots. In 2000, John headed off to CMU in Mt. Pleasant. Steve went to Calvin in 2002, located in Grand Rapids, with Josh to follow in 2004. Poor Matt. He just had Mom and Dad at home. He missed his brothers. We all were adjusting to our shrinking family. God reminded me He never intended us to keep our children. Our job as parents is to grow them with a firm foundation in Christ and to fan the flame He puts within them so that they can move on into the world…for HIS glory! Good in theory, but I so did not want to do it! Not really a choice, more of a heart adjustment and a peeling back of the hands to let go…and then a pounding in of the nails to keep the hands open. It did feel that painful!

What made it worse is Michael lost his job in June of 2004 and could not find full time work until February 2005. He was blessed with several odd jobs, but not enough to pay the bills and especially to cover health insurance. He applied for countless positions, but at 51, he had to stand in line behind many younger men. What about experience? What about maturity? We were confident God would provide a job. Although God was ever faithful to provide, no job was in sight. At the end of October our insurance ran out. It was even harder to try to get other insurance with two pre-existent conditions; Matt's seizures and my Porphyria (more on that later). With his heart in his throat and great sadness in his eyes, Michael came to me and said he thought I would need to go back to work. He felt like a failure to provide as a husband and father. Not true, but he "felt" like it. I had asked him off and on throughout this time about me looking for work, but he knew our desire to have me home and always said "No." I did not argue as I did not want to work. At the time, Matt was a freshman in high school. Although he was more than fine being at home by himself, my heart broke to think of losing precious time with him. I also was struggling big time with anger at Michael being out of work and me having to work. Totally selfish. I had been free to stay home ALL this time and now when I was needed, I balked. My Mom was still alive but not mentally able to give me her words of wisdom I so wanted to hear to confirm what I knew I needed to do. She would have said, "Susan, this is a season in your life. Family does whatever is necessary to function. You have been blessed for a very long time to stay home with your boys. Now you need to work. God will watch over Matt, He always has."

I started looking for jobs. I did not want to work retail with evening/weekend hours. I had a degree in Social Work and Psychology but without a Masters, it was pretty much useless. I asked God for a great paying job that would pay benefits from 10:00–2:00, Monday–Friday. I knew He was able. But God said no. I actually was offered a job cleaning at a Christian Assisted Living Residence in Lansing. On my way home, I was thanking God for the position but I was heavy hearted.

As I drove, I was doing what I always do...looking at houses and property. Hello?!!! What about being a Realtor? I confess my confidence was low. Even though I had always had an interest in real estate, I figured Michael would say I needed to take the offered job. Instead, he encouraged me to take the 40 hour week of real estate classes and to take the exam. He believed in me! My family and friends believed in me and were praying! I loved the classes but also felt overwhelmed with all the information crammed into one week. I took the exam the following Tuesday and failed by 3 points. I was devastated. I dreaded telling my cheerleading family and friends. Michael said, "Try again." I did. I passed. I started working January 3,

2005 for Coldwell Banker Hubbell in Lansing with Matt Bowler as my Broker. It was a tremendous amount of work but it was also wonderfully fun! God blessed me with all kinds of business and I loved it. I was told to be successful, I would need to work 24/7. I thought about that. I prayed about that. I saw God with a little smirk shaking His head. NOT His plan for me with real estate. Again, HE was His plan for me. I felt God saying to me that if I fail at real estate, I do not make money. If I fail at being a wife and mother, I fail. I chose to trust Him…again.

For sure, I had to control my business or it would control me. Daily I would surrender it to God to manage, to bring in business or not. I tried to limit my time working weekends and evenings. One of the many great things about real estate is you are your own boss – and I was a good one! I aimed to work while Matt was at school and Michael at work. I tried to work while they were gone, whether day or night. If Matt had games, I would be there for the game. I also was home to see Matt off to school and Michael off to work in the mornings. I did do my best to be home when Matt got home from school. If we were not at a game, we still had dinners together. I tried to do much of my computer work in the evening while Matt was doing homework and Michael was away. He had started a full time job in February, 2005 in hospital insurance and traveled quite a bit for three years. My ever faithful fans, Michael and Matt were great about cheering me on in my work. It is a huge "no-no" to not do open houses on Sundays in the Lansing area. I went to my Broker, also a Christian, and explained I did not plan to do them. He told me it was my business, my choice. I had MANY Realtors tell me I HAD to do open houses or I would be ruined in my business. I chose to trust God. Most of my wonderful clients were fine with me not doing open houses, but a few asked me to have them. I would not miss church, so about a dozen times out of the 3 ½ years I was active in real estate, I honored those requests on Sunday afternoons. God brought in business and I wanted all to know it was because of Him I was successful. On the back of my business card, with permission from my Broker, I put:

I work hard
I pray harder
Putting you in THE best of Hands
Buy or sell with me and I will give
10% of my commission to the
Christian organization of your choice
I look forward to working with you!

I had some cross key chains made up. They were bigger than I planned and looked like potty passes – I still have plenty, want one? I also had emery boards with a little house shape and a Christian fishy symbol printed on them. I had one jerky Realtor tell me I could not say anything about being a Christian. I told him it was my business, and I could. He walked away in a huff. I have to admit, sad but true, I enjoyed selling more real estate than him! Every now and then, Michael would need to give me "the look" to help me prioritize. It was a joy to be able to have the freedom to be off work whenever the boys were around and to go visit them sporadically. Also, much of real estate is done on the phone so I could be in Florida with family and still doing business…but that was also a problem…I was still doing business.

Another "season" occurred during that same period. For 25 years I had been a minister's wife. I was still married to a minister, but he was not working in that capacity. I could not believe the range of emotions I dealt with during the time we were not employed in ministry. To free our church family from feeling divided with their allegiance, we began going to another church. I missed my "family." I stayed in touch with many but you know how that goes, "Out of sight, out of mind." I also realized we all had "life" going on and would not see many if not "scheduled" to go to the same activities. When "life" happens, most friends become acquaintances. Truly, we all have only 24 hours to each day and limited energy. I understand that. I too, am limited. To live in the same area and not worship together was strange. I think it would have been easier to have moved to a new area and therefore not expect to see or be together. It was weird going to a church without being in leadership. Our involvement was different. Unfortunately, that church started having problems and eventually split. Families should never split, especially Christian families. God cries out for unity, not division. Satan delights in it.

We began going to still another church, a BIG church with five services; two on Saturday night and three on Sunday. Great teaching and wonderful music but it was, again, strange going some place where no one ever knew if you came. Definitely NOT the reason to go or not to go to church, but there is a "harmony" that cannot occur when you are singing alone. Of course I wondered how I could feel so alone with hundreds all around…that is the worst kind of alone. It was NOT the church's fault I was feeling alone. It was God working on my heart, shaping and molding me into His image. He was giving me a hunger for fellowship, yet reminding me that I am complete in Him. With lights low, I could have come and gone in my house coat and no one would have ever noticed, let alone cared. There is some beauty to that, but not much. What I missed was really knowing people. I liked looking around, knowing how to best pray for them. God reminded me He still knew them and would prompt me to lift up this one or that one. I still felt so disconnected. Maybe I had become too connected to people. I find that hard to believe, but there was some definite distancing that occurred during this time with ones whom I had thought would be life long friends. I had to open my hands and let Him pound in the nails…again. He reminded me that He was the only life long Friend I could anchor into. This distancing did help prepare me for our move to Kalamazoo. In fact, in some ways, the move relieved some of that heartache because I no longer was in physical proximity and so had no hope or expectation of contact. Again, God reminded me He alone was my hope and expectation (Psalms 62:5).

God knows I like closure. He gave me a triple dose. Oakland Drive Christian Church in Kalamazoo had offered Michael the Senior Minister position that began in May, 2007. Part of our agreement with them was for us to stay in Lansing until Matt graduated from high school in June, 2008. They were wonderfully supportive. So that meant Michael commuted from May 2007 until August 2008, willingly, NEVER complaining. God sold our house in an awful market within four months and we closed, emptied our house, and moved our stuff loaded in trucks to the church parking lot – all with the help of FOREVER family and friends. That was on a Monday and we stayed in a hotel until Friday of that week when we moved Matt to college. We came back to close on our new house, and met our church family at the new house to unload everything… all on the same day! It was good and awful all at the same time.

Lots of changes. Change can keep you busy for awhile as you settle in and adapt to God's new season specially designed for you. In addition to everything else going on, our #4 son, Josh graduated from Calvin College the middle of May and accepted a great marketing job in Chicago. With a heavy heart, but rejoicing with Josh, Michael and I moved him from Grand Rapids, 45 minutes away, to Chicago, 2 ½ hours away from Kalamazoo. We also praised God for rewarding all his hard work at Calvin with a desirable job. Our firstborn son, John, married his beloved, Vanessa Smith, July 12 of that year in Wauchula, Florida. We were all there to celebrate with them. Right after we moved to Kalamazoo, our number three angel, Elisabeth Hope, was born on August 28. I was able to fly down again to welcome her and play with her two sisters, Sydney Joy and Madeline Grace. While flying home from there, I was filled with lots of mixed emotions about these changes in my life: a new church and ministry, a new house and neighborhood, an empty nest with all the boys gone, and the need for a new job for me. Although I have kept my real estate license current, I stopped actively selling…for now. The Michigan market has been very difficult since 2007 and I was not familiar with the Kalamazoo area, nor did I have connections here…yet. We shall see if God opens the door in the future. God blessed that "season" in my life and we were thankful!

There is something glorious in starting new things, but in the midst of all the glory came the grief – my "Mom-hood" days were over. Of course I will always be their Mom, but my role had changed. Something said at Matt's graduation really helped me through this time... "Don't cry because it's over, smile because it happened." What a marvelous "season of life!" For me, there has been no better way for me to understand the Fatherhood of God than through parenting. I think parenting is the most selfless act of love ever. I thank Him for the blessed opportunity and priceless gift of being a parent; giving and sharing life with five precious sons. I am thankful that God has entrusted us with loving, teaching, raising, and sending them out into the world. I miss all the time with the boys, our family time. I adore them. We have a marvelous treasure in our boys. What a super season of life! I choose to continue to enjoy each moment we have with them. Instead of calls for permission, the boys will call for prayers, advice, recipes, checking schedules for times together, and to update us on their lives. We are learning to share all over again. Instead of learning to share time with my family and Michael's family, we now are learning to share our kids with their diverse schedules and with their wives' families. They are not ours to own...but to love, pray for, and enjoy! We do not want to miss a chance to do that! What an honor to recognize MUCH MORE each day the blessings God gives us in our unique seasons of life...and to thank Him!

P.S. My Mom was right again; I now have more time! I have entrusted it to my Master Planner!

May these sayings that have encouraged me along my varying seasonal walk encourage you.

■■

No God. No Peace.
Know God. Know Peace.

Look back and thank God. Look forward and trust God. Look around and serve God. Look within and find God.

Don't worry about tomorrow. God is already there.

Life without God is a hopeless end; Life with God is endless hope.

The main thing is to keep the Main Thing the Main Thing.

If we ask "Why me?" with trials, we must ask "Why me?" with blessings.
> Arthur Ash – a tennis pro who died of AIDS due to a blood transfusion

True Worship = Up reach, In reach, Out reach

Faith is a lift, not a load.

Lord, help me to remember that there is nothing that is going to happen today that, together, You and I can't handle.

Praise is the key that frees me to worship. Forgiveness is the key that frees me from the bondage of anger and bitterness.

If I want to be encouraged, I must first encourage. If I want to be understood, I must first take time to understand.

I need to live as if Jesus died yesterday, resurrected today, and is coming back tomorrow!

Jesus came to pay a debt He didn't owe, because we owed a debt we couldn't pay.

People don't care how much you know, until they know how MUCH you care.

Failure is not defeat unless you stop trying.

God does not comfort us to make us comfortable, but to make us comforters.

Safety is not the absence of danger but the presence of God.

Before you talk to men about God, talk to God about men.

The only thing that goes with the flow is dead wood.

Man turns the Rock of Salvation into the quicksand of theology.
Michael J. O'Berski (II Corinthians 11: 3, 4 and Jude 3, 4)

Don't question in the dark what you know to be true in the light.

Interruptions? or **divine appointments**?
Dean Trune

God, plan my blessing, not bless my plans.
Michael J. O'Berski

Philosophy = Men pooling their ignorance.
Michael J. O'Berski

Man measures success by numbers. God measures success by faithfulness. God is responsible for the results.
Gary Hawes

A Bible that is falling apart usually belongs to a person who isn't.
Death = servant to usher us into the arms of the Living God!

Give all to God. You get what you pay for.
Dean Trune

If we are truly humble, no one should be able to humiliate us.

Unless God is Lord of all, He is not Lord at all.
Gary Hawes

World says, "Seeing is believing." God says, "Believing is seeing."

Courage does not always roar. Sometimes it is the quiet voice at the end of the day saying I will try again tomorrow.
Mary Anne Radmacher

You'll miss 100% of the shots you don't take.

Life is not about waiting for the storms to pass. It's about learning to dance in the rain.
Vivian Greene

We cannot direct the wind but we can adjust our sails.

Your attitude will determine your altitude.
Zig Ziglar

Wisdom is knowing the right path to take. Integrity is taking it.

Choice, not chance, determines our destiny.

The road to success is not always a road.

No traffic jams on the extra mile.

Purpose of life is a life of purpose.

We make a living by what we get, we make a life by what we give.
> Winston Churchill

In the middle of every difficulty comes opportunity.
> Albert Einstein

What if faith, not fear, was your default reaction to threats?
> Max Lucado, <u>Fearless</u>

If the tomb of Jesus is empty, then the promise of Jesus is not.
> Max Lucado, <u>Fearless</u>

You are always one choice away from changing your life.

If every circumstance finds us abiding in Christ, we will find Christ abiding with us in every circumstance.

CHAPTER 22

THE ETERNAL ARMS

"The eternal God is your refuge,
and underneath are the everlasting arms."
Deuteronomy 33:27

God is our Alpha and Omega, our beginning and our end. His everlasting arms have been underneath me the whole time as I went through each beginning and end. Many times He carried me, but I still had to go through them. God is always with me and I praise Him. One of my all time favorite passages in the Bible is the 43rd chapter of Isaiah. God tells us He created us and formed us for His glory. He has redeemed us, so not to have fear. I LOVE this part, "I have summoned you by name (Susan!); you are mine." This part I am not quite as crazy apart; "<u>When</u> (not if) you pass through the waters, I will be with you; and <u>when</u> you pass through the rivers, they will not sweep over you. <u>When</u> you walk through the fire you will not be burned; the flames will not set you ablaze." I found myself focusing on WHEN. God knew my thoughts. He said, "Susan, focus on ME, the 'I will be with you' parts." God went on to tell me He is my God, my ONLY Savior, and that I, Susan Ruth O'Berski, am precious in His sight. PRECIOUS! He tells me He loves me and not to be afraid. He reminds me that He has chosen me (ME!) as His servant to be His witness.

"Susan, I want you to know me, believe me, understand me" (verse 10). To think the God of the Universe wants ME to know and understand Him! Wowser!!!

I am sure we all have friends, or shall we call them acquaintances, who are always happy to join us in our good times. There are also friends who will walk with us through some tough times. But it is the true friend who will stay with us no matter what; when the tough times stay tough, to ask the hard questions, to listen even when they do not like what they are hearing. It seems as if human nature has a limit on sadness. You can be sick for two weeks. You can grieve maybe for three months, but then people get tired of asking how you are. Human nature seems to say everything can be "fixed." When it isn't, we do not know what to do. Friends of mine who have had cancer or a chronic illness have mentioned how after awhile, they are left alone. Grieving is so unique to each person I think it best to allow them to set their own time. I ask God to let me know what they need because they usually do not. Then if He says to do something, I do it...make a phone call, say a prayer, send a card, or stop by for a hug. When my parents died I had a couple of friends who regularly sent me cards telling me they were still praying...even at the one year mark. That was HUGE for me. I have tried to do the same for others and I know God has touched hearts with His love because of it. I so remember thinking after my Dad's funeral on the way to the cemetery how all the cars passing us had no clue that my world had stopped. Now I try to pray for the families involved in a funeral procession whenever I see one. Life does go on, but their world has forever been altered. When I hear a police, fire, or ambulance siren I pray, "God be with those in need and those helping." It has become a habit that I believe is a God thing. There is no better time for God to touch a person's very tender, aching soul than amidst tragedy. I did not realize it was actually possible for your heart to really feel like it is breaking. It is. For months after my Dad's death I remember sighing a lot. Sounds silly, I know, but it was like I could not catch my breath and nothing mattered.

For two months, I had no patience for small talk about anything with anyone. Who cared? Not me. I felt sad. I did not care that someone's neighbor's daughter failed a class or that so and so was mad at so and so – so what! My Dad died. I could not focus on anything and yet had to go on with daily routine. Much of that is good but at the time, so very difficult. One day I was having an extremely hard time and my eyes were "leaky." Matt, at age 3, asked me why I was crying. I told him because I loved Grandpa and I missed him so much. At THREE, with the wisdom of a child, he told me, "Mommy, Grandpa still loves you too." I grabbed him and hugged him so hard. God had used my precious little boy to speak to me. God knew I was thinking my relationship with Dad was over, and in human terms, it was. But **God is love** and love never fails; it is eternal, and the love we shared goes on forever. That was the beginning of healing for me. Grieving my loss continued, but I could breathe normally again. I could even smile and not feel guilty. My days up until that point had been consumed with thinking about Dad. I remember the first day I did not think of my Dad once and it scared me that I was going to forget him. No, I was healing.

Everyone is different. I spoke to a co-worker this week whose husband died one year ago and she had struggled so with her loss. A friend had suggested that she write a memorial for his upcoming birthday. She did, and remarked that it had freed her to live again. My Mom died five years ago this coming July and I have missed her more this past month than when she died. A sweet volunteer at our gift shop in the assisted living residence came in right before Mother's Day wearing my Mom's favorite perfume and I teared up. I told her why and when she asked how long my Mom had been gone, I choked up – it had been FIVE years. Many things trigger emotions. Emotions come from God and I believe He wants to use them to sensitize us to others and to Him. The first year after my Mom died I felt guilty that I was not missing her. In losing a parent who has any type of dementia, you "lose" them way before they die. I did not miss the last year of my Mom's life.

The writing of this book has brought so many beautiful memories of her to mind that my "real" Mom is back...and I miss her. But it is a good miss.

God has also used her final years in a beautiful way to tune me in to the families who are caring for their parents at my work place. I understand. We have a couple who both have a type of dementia and, resultantly, are acting out in unpleasant ways. Their family is wonderful and so supportive, but has been so apologetic and embarrassed about some of their parent's unusual practices. God is ever faithful to share with me their needs and to whisper in my ear things He wants me to say to them. I simply said that I wanted them to know that I love their parents. They teared up. I went on to say that our wonderful staff knows these acts are not who their parents really are. They simply said, "Thank you." I am seeing an inkling of the HUGENESS (**still** too small of a word) of God's eternity. I believe that sharing life with Christ means sharing in His many attributes. Wisdom. My wisdom of 56 years does not go very far in contrast to God's ETERNAL wisdom. Seeing that God is ALL about people, I am learning He wants us to tap into His ETERNAL virtues and let HIS SPIRIT touch others through us. It is such an exciting, blessed honor. Ozzie, in Utmost, writes on June 17, "I have never met a person I could despair of, or lose all hope for, after discerning what lies in me apart from the grace of God." God wants to love others through us...will we let Him?

~~~A side note of CAUTION~~~ There are people, too many people, who go through life "grieving" about everything. It is not grieving. Rather, it is moodiness, which I call selfishness. God calls it SIN. They mope around wanting all eyes on them, demanding everyone's sympathy. I used to send our boys to bed if they got moody and tell them they could come out of their room when they had a positive mood instead of an ugly mood. I reminded them it was a choice. No fun to be moody if you do not get the attention you want from it. We so wrongfully use cop outs in our life to proclaim our "right" to be in a bad

mood. Ozzie, on May 20, says, "We blame things on the devil that are actually the result of our own undisciplined natures.... there are certain things in life that we need not pray about – moods, for instance. We will never get rid of moodiness by praying, but we will by kicking it out of our lives."

Talk about undisciplined natures! The other day I ate FIVE (maybe six) spoonfuls of chocolate chip cookie dough...yes, dough does mean uncooked! I was so disgusted with myself. Looking for someone or something to blame besides myself (THE one who crammed it all in my mouth), I told Michael there must be a full moon coming. Now you all know what PMS is, yes? PRE MOON SYNDROME!!!! Do you run and hide when you hear PMS? Do you tremble at the very mention of the term? Every woman on earth knows the feeling and, I am confident, every man and child knows the consequences. I know the term is also known for something else just as fun but, over the years, I have come to notice I am greatly influenced by a full moon – and it is not in a good way. Yet I would rationalize it was okay being nasty due to the full moon. Nasty is always wrong! If I choose to be nasty, I have to take the blame. Tropicana orange juice has little white pull tabs on their half gallons that look like FULL MOONS. I have saved them over the years and shared them with other women to put on their fingers to WARN anyone entering within flame thrower range!!! Pitiful when our loved ones have to wear asbestos suits to survive our moods! Email me at susie.oberski@gmail.com and I will send you your very own moon ring to warn all to stay clear of your gun shot/ear shot. God is God for the good, bad, AND ugly! Run to Him! His everlasting arms are for YOU!
~~~

Back to Isaiah 43:10 with God telling me He wants me to know, believe and understand Him. I decided I wanted to take God at His Word. I wanted to know ALL of God, including the Man of Sorrows. Isaiah 53:3 says, "He was despised and rejected by men; a man of sorrows, and familiar with suffering. Like one from whom men hide their faces, He was despised, and we esteemed Him not." The Man of Sorrows. I do not think of Jesus like that. I think I may have avoided the thought because to focus on the God of Love, Joy, and Peace is much more soothing. I feel ruffled to think God knows sorrow.

I want to share with you some of my journaling from our dark hour struggles. On July 30, 2004, I recorded that I want to know this Man of Sorrows, what a Savior. Hebrews 5:8 says "Tho' He was a Son, yet He learned obedience by the things which He suffered." How can I expect to know Jesus without walking with THE Man of Sorrows? I realize how FAR I have yet to go as I don't count all things but loss so that I might gain Jesus. I count all things precious WITH Jesus. I want my hands full of all, not empty with nails in them. Forgive me, Lord. Whatever, however, help me be all You'd have me to be; to go it alone if necessary. I'm ready to quit instead of pressing on so that I might gain You. Forgive me, help me.

October 1, 2004 found me in **God Calling**, "Look to no other source for Salvation. Only look unto Me. See no other supply…Regard Me as your only supply." My response to that was that truly, You are my only supply, Lord. Thank You. Thank You for reminding me as I came to You this morning and asked You to speak to me. I am so struggling with anger at Michael for letting our health insurance run out – I feel vulnerable. Matt and I have preexistent "conditions." YET, **You are my ONLY supply** – my only constant; NOT Michael, insurance, jobs, health, friends – YOU! Help me rest in You. Help me joy in You. **YOU ONLY**. (I must add here that Michael WAS caring best for us in that if you do not have money, you do not spend money. I was desperately seeking a "savior" other than God, my ONLY SUPPLY.)

On October 4, 2008, I journaled that we had dinner with friends who are good, kind people who have been hurt by various churches. I struggle with Christians who hold onto their hurt. Everyone gets hurt – that is life. If we become cautious, afraid we'll get hurt again, where does that put us? Behind walls. What if Jesus had stopped when He was hurt? He would still be hanging on a tree, DEAD – like us when we stop because we're afraid we'll get hurt again. We need to recognize that hurt comes with life, that we need to leave the pain at the cross, step forward and move on. How else can God use us? My hope **is** in Christ, not man. I referenced John 2:24, "But Jesus would not entrust Himself to them, for He knew all men." Jesus knew His hope was in God Who knew Him totally, loved Him eternally, and held Him in His everlasting arms. So is ours.

Why do I let man disappoint me so? Cling to Jesus, our forever Friend! God Calling, on October 26, specifically spoke to me when I was experiencing such a distancing from my "known" world at the time. Jesus is speaking, "I am so often wounded in the house of My friends. Do you think the spitting and scorn of My enemies, the mocking and reviling hurt me? No! It is not the unbelief of My enemies that hurts, but that My friends, who love and know Me, cannot walk all the way with Me, and doubt My power to do ALL that I have said."

On December 4, 2008 I recorded how our Josh was hurt by a dear friend he had graduated from Calvin with seven months earlier. This friend shared that he felt a need to break off ties with his old friends so that he could make new friends. With his unabashed tenacity to loyalty in friendship, Josh responded with, "If I can't be your old friend, can I be your new friend?" I LOVE THAT! Such a heart for his friends – so like Jesus! Instead of choosing to be hurt and resentful, Josh was willing and wanting to try again, to be a forever friend. Yeah, Joshie!!!

I am reminded that JESUS and my RELATIONSHIP with Him ALONE is my goal, my purpose. The goal is NOT the destination, it is the journey with God by my side. God ALONE can and will go with me all the way; HE is eternal, He is everlasting. His everlasting arms of love will wrap around me and hold me up forever. EVERLASTING and FOREVER is a very long time. Lord, help me to listen to You and thrive on Your smile alone. I choose to trust You, thanking You for being with me each step of every day.

We will have wilderness days, but these too will pass. Jesus survived 40 days of fasting as He journeyed through the wilderness **because** He was **led by the Spirit** (John 4:1). We must be too. This Man of Sorrows, Who passed through the deepest depths of sorrows while hanging on the cross with our sin separating Him from God, also experienced the highest heights of exhilaration in God's presence on the Mount of Transfiguration. God IS my song in the night (Job 35:10). God knows what lies in darkness, and Light dwells with Him (Daniel 2:22). Though I sat in darkness, the Lord was my Light. He brought me out into the light and promised me I would see His righteousness (Micah 7:8, 9). The Lord turned my darkness into light (II Samuel 22:29). God is ever present to be your Light in the darkness too.

The song, **"Let the Waters Rise"** by **Mikeschair** speaks of those times in our lives when we feel our world is caving in and we desperately cry out for help but see no relief. Throughout the song, we are reminded God never leaves us. His love IS enough. **HIS LOVE IS ENOUGH.**

The **ETERNAL GOD** IS our refuge in good times and bad. His EVERLASTING arms are there to hold us…to lift us up. **God has SO MUCH MORE for us as we seek to know Him more and more.** Ask Him to show you **He is enough, MUCH MORE than enough.**

CHAPTER 23

LET PEACE RULE

"Let the peace of God rule in your hearts, since as members of one body you were called to peace."
Colossians 3:15

We live in a take charge society and I am a take charge person. It is hard for me to let go, to surrender leadership to "just" anyone. They have to prove themselves to me and I have some pretty tough qualifications. God has proven Himself to me over and over again so the easiest leaders for me to follow are those who are following God. However, I still know I am to pray for all leaders, and trust God to work through them. In fact, that is a huge factor in my having peace in everyday life. **I CHOOSE to LET the PEACE of GOD RULE** in my heart. I look to God, obey Him, and trust Him to lead me, in everything.

My Dad used to think you should not bother God with all of the "little" stuff, that God was too busy. I disagreed and told him I believed God wants to be involved in every aspect of our lives including where to go to school, what friends to invest my life in, whom to marry, what job to take, and even in finding me a parking place. When you choose to surrender your life to Christ and take Him seriously, He takes you seriously. Knowing that God is ordering your day with His great wisdom and mercy is the epitome of peace.

Let me give you an example with job hunting. When Michael and I were first married in 1977, he was working part time and going to Great Lakes Bible College (now Great Lakes Christian College) in Lansing. He was quite busy adding Bible classes to his undergraduate degree from MSU while interning with Gary Hawes of His House. We knew until he completed his two year course work at GLBC, I would need to work full time. We were both great with that. Great, until I was not able to get the job I wanted.

After all, I was spoiled and had always gotten everything I wanted; why would that stop now?!!! I had interviewed for a secretarial position in the Philosophy Department at MSU and was offered the job. I thanked them and said I would need to pray about it and talk to my husband about it. I did not tell them I had my dream job awaiting me and they were not it! Having graduated with a double major in Social Work and Psychology, I had dreamed of working with troubled teens, and possibly in the school system. That very job was advertised, I had applied, and they were beginning interviews in TWO weeks. No problem. I knew when I went home from my interview and told my new and wonderful husband (I love that word, husband!) that, of course, he would say for his darling wife to wait for whatever her little heart wanted. WRONG! He reminded me that we had already prayed and had asked God for a full time job with benefits. God had answered that prayer. BUT, I reminded him, in TWO WEEKS I will probably get my dream job! Probably was just not good enough when we had a definite job in hand by just reaching out for it. This "darling" wife was not feeling so darling and not quite so fond of the word, husband! Hmmmpfh! Yoohoo, Booboo! Remember, I have a degree! Michael seemed to think that a job in hand was worth a bush full of degrees! I confess a rotten attitude and a snobbery of superiority BUT I knew he was right. I also knew Michael was a man of God and that I could submit to his wisdom BECAUSE he was following God, and I could trust

God. Michael had not proven himself to me like God had, but I chose to trust God to lead through Michael. With that came great peace and a confirmation in the job that God wanted me right where HE was putting me – in a department full of (mostly) atheistic philosophers and graduate students. God reminded me jobs are about people and where HE needs us to ECHO HIS GLORY. Degrees can open doors, but God is the key. If HIS key does not fit, I do not want the job! That one hard lesson paved the way for God to choose our jobs from then on. By the way, I was never called for my dream job.

Truly, there is great peace when you surrender every decision to God. Whether it is jobs, schools, houses, vacations, whether to invest in this or that, or the timing on talking with someone and the words to go with that talk, God wants to be involved. We now pray for God to open wide the doors He wants us to go through, and nail shut any doors He does not want us to go through…and we rest. Mostly. Okay, we know we should rest; we still sometimes struggle and go back to God and make sure He heard us right. His hearing is ALWAYS good, it is mine that is not.

Another example is when we were moving from my favorite home and area of Brighton to Mt. Pleasant. We had looked for a full day at houses and found nothing. I was miserable all the way home. The next time we found my most favorite house right on a gorgeous acre lot AND a river. Custom built. We both loved it! We put an offer on it and I knew we were going to get it because that would make me happy and our move to that "foreign" land so much easier. WRONG AGAIN! Of course we had prayed that silly "nail shut/swing wide" prayer and God had taken us seriously. God also reminded me that although He does like me happy, He is MUCH MORE concerned with my character than my happiness. Can't I have both?! Nope! Not if I am going to have an attitude! We did not get the house and I was devastated! I am learning to save my drama of devastation for things that really matter, like people, not houses. We found another house, with the best neighbors ever! A year later we found that my dream house had flooded in the spring and had been destroyed. God said, "Susan, NOW will you trust Me?" **Trusting God releases peace. Trusting God to lead you wherever He wants you to go, frees you to follow with HIS peace, HIS joy.**

I love the passage in Scripture that shows us one of the many ways God lead His people of Israel. God shows us how to follow His lead. Not only did He use a cloud by day to lead and protect, that cloud "looked like fire" by night. God does not want us to miss what He wants for us! We have an awesome God Who desires to be involved in our lives. He does whatever it takes to get our attention so we can be involved in HIS life!

> *"On the day the tabernacle, the Tent of the Testimony, was set up, the cloud covered it. From evening till morning the cloud above the tabernacle looked like fire. That is how it continued to be; the cloud covered it, and at night it looked like fire. Whenever the cloud lifted from above the Tent, the Israelites set out; wherever the cloud settled, the Israelites encamped. AT THE LORD'S COMMAND, the Israelites set out, and AT HIS COMMAND they encamped. As long as the cloud stayed over the tabernacle, they remained in camp. When the cloud remained over the tabernacle a long time, the Israelites obeyed the Lord's order and did not set out. Sometimes the cloud was over the tabernacle only a few days; AT THE LORD'S COMMAND they would encamp, and then AT HIS COMMAND they would set out. Sometimes the cloud stayed only from evening till morning, and when it lifted in the morning, they set out. Whether by day or by night, WHENEVER the cloud lifted, they set out. Whether the cloud stayed over the tabernacle for two days or a month or a year, the Israelites would remain in camp and not set out; but when it lifted, they would set out. AT THE LORD's COMMAND they encamped, and AT*

THE LORD's COMMAND *they set out. They obeyed the Lord's order." Numbers 9:15-23*

Are we that willing to come and go **at His command**, willing to obey His directions? Do we ask for His leading? Do we follow? Or do we follow just when it suits our fancy? When it is comfortable or convenient? His leading did not stop with the Old Testament or with Christ's ascension. We have His Holy Spirit. His Word is active and sharper than any double-edged sword (Hebrews 4:12). God is the Great I AM, the Alpha and Omega, omnipresent, omnipotent, our Shepherd Who leads us through every valley, over every plain, and surmounting every mountain.

For years I wrestled with different sicknesses and my parents were ever patient in caring for me. I am sure Kaye, Scott, and Patti got tired of me always being sick. Me too! Everything lasted longer than it "should." I had ear aches, sore throats with eventual tonsillectomy, stomach pain, appendectomy, and Mononucleosis twice. What seemed to be typical childhood illnesses extended into adulthood with complications. Additionally, five breast biopsies (all thankfully benign), three laparoscopies (back to the stomach/side pain), kidney stone and removal (OUCH!), hysterectomy, and I still have solar carcinoma spots removed regularly…just call me Spot! As my dear sister Patti says, I am very healthy except for being so sickly. ☺

The first six months of our marriage was incident free. Then I started feeling sick everyday with nausea, side pain, and exhaustion. I could have slept anytime, anywhere, anyplace. But I could not; I needed to work. So at lunch time I would go to the MSU Union building next door, eat a bagel and yogurt and take a nap. My sweet Dad told Michael the warranty was up and I was all his. Thankfully, we had good insurance and my boss in the Philosophy Department was extremely supportive and concerned. I started going to a doctor who sent me to this doctor who sent me to that doctor…and on and on it went. The good news is that they could find nothing. The bad news is they could find nothing. I was discouraged and felt like maybe it was all in my head, even tho' I did not really think so. I hated being sick, especially as a new wife. Michael was discouraged because he could not "fix" his wife. (Still can't ;) I hated for his parents to know but we finally went to Dad O'Berski, who was an Osteopathic Doctor. He wisely listened and kindly suggested I go off of the birth control pills I had started taking three months before our wedding. In about two weeks, I started feeling better. We were hopeful, and then, surprise…I got pregnant with John! How excited and thankful we were! The timing seemed perfect because Michael was going to graduate in May, 1979 and Johnny was not due until September. Our exhilaration covered over my ALL DAY morning sickness that lasted "only" the first five months. I ended up in the hospital the day after Michael's graduation party with a high fever and severe pain, discovering a kidney infection. I had not felt well, but did not want to distract from Michael's celebration. Thankfully, the baby was not affected. After a week in the hospital, I was back to work.

With plans to help start a new His House campus ministry on the University of Michigan campus, God opened the door for Michael at the UM Hospital as a Manager of Housekeeping with Service Master. We packed up and moved there in June, 1979. God also provided me with a three month secretarial job in the Psychology Department and then I graduated becoming MOM on September 30, 1979!

This story goes on and on with continued doctor appointments looking for the source of my pain, nausea, and exhaustion. Praise God, I seemed to feel best while pregnant, and except for the kidney infection with Johnny, was very healthy with all five pregnancies. Finally in 1997, I went to my parent's doctor, an amazing diagnostician. He listened to me and looked over all the x-rays and doctor reports I had taken to him. He told me to go back to my family doctor and have him test me for four things. I do not even remember the other three, but the fourth one was a very rare genetic blood disease, Porphyria. (Do not drop this book, I am not contagious!

;) I believe it is rare only because doctors are not familiar with it and do not test for it. Sure enough, I had it!

Now the whole reason I have taken you through this very long treatise is to get you to this point: JESUS. He is always the point! My doctor, who was not crazy about having another doctor tell him what to test me for, obliged. He called me and asked me to come into his office. Michael was at work. The boys were old enough to stay home alone with Matt so I jumped in the car and drove to his office. He sat me down and explained that the test had proven conclusively that I had Porphyria. He told me a little about the disease, Hereditary Coproporphyria (HCP), considered one of at least eight porphyrin disorders which result from a deficiency in specific enzymes along the heme biosynthetic pathway. It sounds crazy, but as he listed the many symptoms, I felt relief…this was not all in my head. He continued to say there was no cure but there were things I could do to help manage the disease. I was excited! THEN, he said it can be life threatening, even fatal. After that, I did not hear much more.

Alone, all I could think of on the way home was FATAL. I cried out to God and reminded Him I was the mother of FIVE wonderful sons who needed me and I needed them! Yes, I was ready for Heaven, but not READY for Heaven! I wanted to enjoy several more years here on Earth. After fifteen minutes of carrying on like this, God took over. He reminded me LIFE IS FATAL. Everyone is going to die. Death is part of life. BUT, and **this is the thing that grabbed my heart, "NOTHING HAS CHANGED. I AM STILL WITH YOU. You have lived with this disease since birth and you will live with this disease until death. This may have rattled your cage, but it has not knocked Me off of my Throne. I REMAIN IN CHARGE! NOTHING HAS CHANGED except you now know what you have…ME!"**

Another great song by **Hosanna/Integrity with Darlene Zschech is "Let the Peace of God Reign."** In the song we are reminded to stand upon God's Truth, allowing His Spirit to **saturate** our soul – oh how I want to saturate my soul with

JESUS! The very word LET points to it being our CHOICE! **We choose** how much of Jesus we have living and breathing in us daily. I want to choose to **LET PEACE RULE!**

   My Proven Peace – God! When you have a proven, trust-worthy (understatement, for sure!) leader to follow, peace reigns. True enough, I still have Porphyria, but I have some-thing SO MUCH better – **the peace of God**. Naturally, I have since researched Porphyria and tried this and that. Some things help, some do not. I do see God's hand of protection throughout my life with this disease because I have never been attracted to some of the things that are most detrimental to Porphyria, alcohol and barbiturates. As hormones run havoc with Porphyria, the one thing that really aggravated my condi-tion was using birth control pills at the beginning of our mar-riage. Learning what to eat and what not to eat is extremely helpful and I even discovered eating ICE CREAM is actually good for me!!! Now how can I not know that God loves me?!! **SO MUCH and MORE!!!**

For more information on Porphyria, contact:
The American Porphyria Foundation
PO Box 22712, Houston, Texas 77227
Telephone: (713) 266-9616
Email: porphyrus@aol.com
Website: www.porphyriafoundation.com

Also in print:
Porphyria, A Lyon's Share of Trouble
Desiree Lyon Howe

CHAPTER 24

REST ASSURED WHILE BEING NAILED TO THE CROSS

"The peace of God, which transcends
ALL understanding.
will guard your heart and your minds
In Christ Jesus."
Philippians 4: 7

T he very title makes me want to say OUCH! Once again, I was planning on writing two chapters on this, but strongly felt God wanting me to combine them. After all, Who could rest assured while being nailed to the cross? Jesus. I am not saying He was without excruciating pain and distress, we know He was. Nor was Jesus free of care. We know He bore the sins of the world and the greatest sorrow of all sorrows being separated from His Father. But Jesus did rest assured while being nailed to the cross BECAUSE He knew He had accomplished what He had been sent to do – to be obedient to His Father and save the world!

It is easy to rest assured as you swing in a hammock under beautiful shade trees on a gorgeous Michigan summer day with a gentle breeze blowing and birds singing. What is not easy is to rest assured while the world around you attacks. But Shadrach, Meshach and Abednego did. In Daniel 3, it is recorded that King Nebuchadnezzar commanded these men to worship his gods or be thrown in a fiery furnace. In verses 16–18 they replied to the king, "We do not need to defend ourselves before you in this matter. If we are thrown into the blazing furnace, **the God we serve IS ABLE** to save us from it, and He will rescue us from your hand, O king. BUT, EVEN IF HE DOES NOT, we want you to know, O king, that we will not serve your gods or worship the image of gold you have set up." Shadrach, Meshach and Abednego knew without a doubt their God was able, **MUCH MORE than able**, to save them. They also knew they had surrendered the rights of their lives to Him as their King and trusted Him to act on their behalf for their best. Either way, they win. If they lived, they lived. If they died, they still lived. It was all in God's hands.

Adoption is part of Kingdom living! So, I "adopt" family wherever I go, with or without their permission. My "Mom", with the same name as my Mom, Fran, shared with me about her two sons going mountain climbing in Colorado right after the older one's divorce. The younger one talked the older one into it by playing the "time of bonding" trump card. Indeed, they had the time of their lives. But it also happened to be the end of life for the older brother. Upon their descent, he slipped and fell, crashing to the depths below. The younger brother cautiously rushed to his side, only to see the fall had been fatal. Alone, in the midst of guilt and despair, he picked him up and carried him to the bottom of the mountain. Upon arrival, he called their Mom and Dad and told them the horror story. Amidst their heartbreak, they tried to console their younger son and release him from his guilt. Her comfort comes from the assurance that her son had trusted Jesus as his Savior and that she would see him again someday in Heaven.

I have a precious new friend, Crystal, who is showing me how to rest assured while being nailed to a cross, a cross of great sorrow. She, too, lost a son, but to the consequences of an alcoholic lifestyle. Due to choices he made, his life ended sooner than necessary. Thankfully, he had turned from alcohol to Jesus, but his body had been irreparably damaged. Her peace comes from Psalm 18:16–19, "He reached down from on high and took hold of me; He drew me out of deep waters. He rescued me from my powerful enemy, from my foes, who were too strong for me. They confronted me in the day of my disaster, BUT **THE LORD WAS MY SUPPORT**. He brought me out into a spacious place; He rescued me because He delighted in me." She wears the following saying on a heart around her neck: Sorrow Looks Back, Worry Looks Around, Faith Looks Up. Crystal shared this has helped her NOT dwell in the past with regrets, anger, or blame as she knows God tells us in John 15 to **dwell in Him**. Her comfort is knowing her son was ready to meet the Lord. Although she and her husband prayed for their son's physical healing, God has assured her that sometimes that prayer of healing is answered in His presence with ultimate healing. Her son is in God's presence in Heaven. She rests in this promise.

For sure, one of the all time worst things to let envelope you in grief, anger, or doubt is hindsight. Hindsight destroys you as it eats away at today. Satan loves to attack the peace of someone with all the "What ifs???" It is impossible to change a thing in the past. We do, however, have the choice of how we look at things and how we will respond. God tells us in Psalms 105:4 to **seek HIS face daily**. Hindsight blinds you. **God sight** clears the fog and gives you insight…**seeing God in all of life!**

Chris Tomlin helps us see God in life AND death through his song, **"I WILL RISE."** He talks about Jesus conquering death victoriously and the peace that comes in knowing Him, the **ANCHOR OF OUR SOUL**. The focus is on rising with Jesus, not dying. Hebrews 4 repeatedly tells us that there is a promise of rest for the people of God. We are reassured by God in Hebrews 6:19 that "We have this hope (in JESUS!) as an anchor for the soul, firm and secure." The best way to **REST ASSURED** throughout this ever changing life is to **grab hold of JESUS, our firm and secure ANCHOR.**

Recently, I have had some disappointment in some dear, older Christians. Older in age, that is. I know, I have said I do not put my hope in man (or woman!) because ONLY God will never disappoint me. Indeed, He is my Hope. However, I do find myself having expectations in older Christians. As my hubby says, older does not necessarily mean mature. True that! Just a couple of weeks ago we encountered a couple different incidents that surprised us with some of my favorite people. I do not expect perfection from Christians, but I do expect them to know the Truth and to act upon it. I even give them room for their first reaction to be human, but their second reaction should be Godly. That is what surprises me when they refuse to do what God commands: to love, to pray, to forgive. Why is it that we all want grace but refuse to give it?!!!

At work one afternoon, I had a dear lady come in to tell me that another woman had come up to her table at lunch time and called her a "witch." I told her to consider the source. She said she did not have the right to say that. I told her she has the right to say it, but that it is **not** "right." Then she told me it was wrong and that woman should not be living at our Christian facility. I looked at her funny and reminded her our job as Christians is to reach out to the world and if we will not do it, who will? She did not care, it was NOT going to be her. I then was a little more bold. I did not really think of it as bold as much as obvious, reminding her our job is to love and pray for others. She got furious and said she would NOT pray for her. I told her we need to pray to ask God to help her forgive this woman. Again, she said she would NOT forgive her. I told her, "Shame on you." I reminded her in not obeying God she is giving Satan the victory and that breaks God's heart. She marched out of the office. I prayed. The next day she returned after breakfast and was in tears. She said the woman had come over to her table and stood right by her saying, "Witch, witch, witch." I almost laughed because I felt I was back in elementary school. I wanted to remind her names don't break her bones, sticks and stones do. But then she was crying. Argh! Okay, I needed to be tender. (I think I have mentioned

MERCY is not my middle name…right boys? I can be merciful IF someone deserves it, but then I do not think that is called mercy. When someone is selfishly stubborn, the LAST thing I want to do is give them any mercy. Again, I sigh and say ARGH!) I went over to her and put my arms around her and told her I loved her and would be praying for God to take care of this - which really meant for her to grow up!

The problem here was she thought she had rights. Whoever said we have rights? Okay, The United States Constitution says we have unalienable "rights"…but that is only if we are NOT aliens – and God says we ARE "aliens and strangers in the world" (I Peter 2:11). Given, some of us are stranger than others…but seriously! IF someone is surrendered to Jesus, we give up ALL rights. That is, after all, the meaning of surrender. God says in Romans 6 that we are dead to sin, alive in Christ. If we are dead, we do not feel anything. If we cannot feel anything, why in the world do we let anything and everything bother us so much?!!! And if we are alive in Christ, God says in Romans 6: 16-18, 22, & 23:

> *"Don't you know that when you offer yourselves to someone to obey him as slaves, you are slaves to the one whom you obey – whether you are slaves to sin, which leads to death, or to obedience, which leads to righteousness. But thanks be to God that, though you used to be slaves to sin, you wholeheartedly obeyed the form of teaching to which you were entrusted. **You have been SET FREE FROM SIN** and have become SLAVES TO RIGHTEOUSNESS…the benefit you reap leads to HOLINESS, and the RESULT IS ETERNAL LIFE. For the wages of sin is death, but the GIFT of God is ETERNAL LIFE in Christ Jesus our LORD."*

The definition of LORD is a person who has authority, control, or power over others; a master, chief, ruler. Do we really want to die to sin **AND** die to ourselves when we choose Jesus as Savior and Lord? Or do we only want the result, eternal life? If we continue to fight for our rights, who is really on the throne? Not Jesus.

We can rest assured in Jesus, not our rights. Rights put our attention on ourselves and what we deserve…also known as SELF righteousness. That is never of God. God alone is righteous and deserves our focus and attention. Satan loves to draw our eyes and heart away from God, usually very subtly. God alone can meet our needs. Psalm 23 tells us with Him as our Shepherd, we will need nothing! Nothing! That pretty much means EVERYTHING we NEED is provided by God. If something is not provided, it must be a want, not a need. Maybe the question we need to ask ourselves is if God really is our Shepherd? Are we following Him? Do we want our rights more than Jesus? When we surrender ALL to God, do we realize that includes ALL – our sins, wants, and rights? God says our sins have been nailed to the cross (Colossians 2). I find that when I start to climb back on the throne of MY righteousness and demand MY rights, I am pounding the nails into Jesus myself. Instead, I need to personally envision myself on the cross with my hands being nailed wide open, able to hold nothing…nothing. **All I need is Jesus. He is more than enough, MUCH MORE THAN ENOUGH!**

Something I have kept in my Bible for years is something Don Finto said at Brighton Christian Church years ago. "If you are not aggressively righteous, you will become passively wicked. People of God, I admonish you: Be a Godly man, a Godly woman. Be a Godly man, a Godly woman of destiny. Away with apathy, lethargy! Be gone with 'letting life happen!' Instead, receive humble, bold servanthood authority of the Lord and accept the responsibility He has given you for your life."

Another incident that occurred happened with a small group of people who got upset with each other over how something was done differently than they thought it should be. None of it was wrong, just different than their own personal preferences. Amazingly, and so sadly, this grew way out of proportion and became a divisive issue that needed to be dealt with for rec-

onciliation. The meeting seemed to go well and after the concluding prayer, there were buddy hugs and everyone went
home. The next day we found out everything was NOT okay.
Something was said in the meeting that was hurtful. When
confronted, the person who had said it acknowledged being
wrong and apologized, asking forgiveness. Some forgave, a
few would not. How can we EVER deny forgiveness? That is
scary to me because Jesus commands us to forgive. In fact,
He states very clearly in the **BE**attitudes, "If you forgive men
when they sin against you, your Heavenly Father will also
forgive you. BUT, IF you do not forgive men their sins, your
Father will NOT forgive your sins" (Matthew 6:14-15). What
happens if we are not forgiven? Scary thought. We cannot
control others, but we can determine what we will do. "As far
as it depends on YOU, live at peace with everyone" (Romans
12:18). God holds US responsible. What will we do with that?
Will we choose to be "aggressively righteous?"

Sometimes, like Job, all we know is that **OUR REDEEMER
LIVES** (Job 19:25) and we need to **CHOOSE to ACTIVELY
REST** in that promise. ACTIVELY REST for sure is an oxy-
moron and is only possible with Jesus. Another favorite senior
saint came into my office the other day and spoke about
having the eye doctor tell her there was really nothing more
that could be done for her eyesight, nor for her Glaucoma.
I said I was sorry and how hard that must be to hear. She
quickly smiled and said with confidence, "Oh no, Honey, that
just means it is the time God steps in and He has ALWAYS
met my needs!" She was assuredly resting in Jesus!

A favorite devotional my husband and I use is **Our Daily
Bread**. April 6, 2010 had a special story that is so applicable
to resting assured in Jesus.

"In an evangelistic meeting in Ireland, the speaker was
explaining what it means to abide in Christ and to trust
Him completely in every trial. Concluding his message,
he repeated several times, "It means that in every cir-

cumstance you can keep on saying, 'For this I have Jesus.'"

The meeting was then opened for testimonies. One young woman said, "Just a few minutes ago I was handed this telegram. It reads, 'Mother is very ill; take train home immediately." When I saw those words, I knew that tonight's message was meant just for me. My heart looked up and said, "For this I have Jesus." Instantly a peace and strength flooded my soul."

Three or four weeks later the evangelist received a letter from this woman. It read, "Thank you again for the message you gave that day. Life has become an uninterrupted psalm of victory, for I have come to realize that no matter what life brings, for this I have Jesus."

Most times we have more questions than we have answers. **For this we have Jesus.** In most trials, we have more problems than we see solutions. **For this we have Jesus.** When doctors say they can do nothing more, watch for God to step in and do more...even if it is "simply" giving you peace with the outcome. Learn to rest in His arms, **assured of Who He is and Whose you are.** After all, Jesus tells us, "See, I have engraved you on the palms of my hands" (Isaiah 49:16). How do you think He got you engraved in His palms? By being nailed to the cross! Not only can we **REST ASSURED** as the eternal God carries us securely in His everlasting arms, but He carries us forever in His hands, having made a way for us to Heaven by being THE WAY, nailed to the cross. Jesus died for us! **Jesus is SO MUCH and MORE! WE ARE HIS MUCH MORE!!!**

CHAPTER 25

FREELY GIVEN

"Give, and it will be given to you.
A good measure, pressed down, shaken together
and running over, will be poured into your lap.
For with the measure you use, it will be measured to you."
Luke 6:38

Nail scarred hands tell us Jesus gave His all; His life for our life. What measure do we use when we give? Do we give freely as it has been given to us? Do we give? Are we an open vessel for God to pour His Spirit through us with our finances, time, and talents? Do we hoard what is given so freely? Maybe that is part of the problem…we think of everything as being "ours." Ozzie says on September 7,

> "We are to be fountains through which Jesus can flow as 'rivers of living water' in blessing to everyone. Yet some of us are like the Dead Sea, always receiving but never giving, because our relationship is not right with the Lord Jesus…STAY AT THE SOURCE, closely guarding your faith in Jesus Christ and your relationship to Him, and there will be a steady flow into the lives of others with no dryness or deadness whatsoever."

We have all heard it is better to give than receive. Where do you think that came from? Probably receivers with their hands held out! But the truth is it comes from givers, starting with Jesus! Those who have experienced the joy and blessing of giving are the ones to listen to, not the Dead Sea worshipers. God tells us in I Corinthians 2:12, "We have not received the spirit of the world but the Spirit Who is from God, (so) that we may understand what God has FREELY GIVEN us." God hands out the spiritual and material food and wants us to pass on our blessings to others. MUCH of God's many miracles happen when we pass on what has been given to us. The feeding of the 5000 happened because a little boy shared his lunch with Jesus. Could Jesus have done it without him? Of course, but He desires to work through us, with us. God is all about TEAMWORK! Could He have turned the water into wine at the wedding feast without His Momma telling Him they were out of wine? Absolutely! But God wants us to come to Him and lay our petitions for ourselves and others at His feet. God Calling on May 24 states, "Abundance is God's supply. Turn out all limited thoughts. Receive showers and in your turn - shower!"

We are a possessive and greedy people. We like to hold onto whatever we have and still reach out for more. For some reason, we think everything we have is ours and everything everyone else has SHOULD be ours. Ownership. Dangerous! When you own something, you are responsible for it. That is one of the MANY reasons it is far better to give back everything to God; then HE is responsible for it!

What boggles my mind is that God owns everything anyway. Why do we claim ownership? Both Psalms 24:1 and Deuteronomy 10:14 say, "The earth is the Lord's and everything in it, the world, and ALL who live in it." Deuteronomy 10:15 continues, "YET the Lord set His affection on your forefathers and loved them, and He chose YOU!" Wowser! Why when God asks us to tithe on all He gives us do we balk? He asks for just 10% and allows us to keep 90% - much better than the government. We even tip those who wait upon us

WE are the MUCH MORE!!!

15–20%. God tells us in Leviticus 27:30 that we are to give a tithe of everything! Michael and I believe that means we tithe on our gross income, not our net income. For us, it needs to come off of the top…that is the "measure" we use. Do we have to? No, we get to!

~~~Side note: Christians, if you get good service or not, PLEASE be generous when you go out to eat and show off your giving God. I have heard way too many waitresses say they hate Sunday because of "All those Christians who, IF they tip, tip low or just leave you one of 'those' tracts." PLEASE be an attraction TO God, not a deterrent FROM God.

A sign of the times came in a letter years ago to my sister, Kaye, from her church. It said that they recognized tithing was difficult so **they** had "established a new tithing" of 3% for their members. I laughed and told Kaye a tithe = 10, a tithe does NOT = 3. Who are we to "establish" a new tithe? Far better to obey the original order for tithing and watch God bless your socks off! You cannot out give God!

God's desire is to remind us EVERYTHING is His and He has chosen to share it all with us. Years ago, some friends from His House at U of M, Mark and Michelle, came to under-stand God's heart behind tithing. They had come face to face with Malachi 3:8–10: "Will a man rob God? Yet you rob Me. But you ask, how do we rob You? In tithes and offerings. You are under a curse – the whole nation of you – because you are robbing Me. Bring the whole tithe into the storehouse, that there may be food in My house. Test Me in this, says the Lord Almighty, and see if I will not throw open the floodgates of Heaven and pour out so much blessing that you will not have room enough for it."

It grieved them that they had not tithed on all of their earn-ings for several years and they wanted to do so, including the interest that would have accumulated over that time period. NOT out of obligation but from joyful hearts, they gave the campus ministry over $25,000. God loves a joyful giver! It has been fun to watch how He has continued to bless them with "good measure, pressed down, shaken together and running over!!!"

Jehovah Jireh is one of God's many names meaning "The Lord will provide." In raising five sons on one salary, and that being a minister's, we had to look to God to provide. Granted, we chose for me to stay home and raise our boys. We also chose for Michael to follow God's leading into the ministry – NO COMPLAINTS, only praises! What an honor to be in His service! Nevertheless, we did have to wait on God often to provide. We saw God bless us abundantly through both sets of parents. We saw God provide money to buy used cars that He kept running far longer than one might expect. We listened to my Dad and ate a lot of pasta and bread to fill our boys ☺ instead of steak and deli food. Our brand-named foods were Meijers and Spartan and we never went hungry.

Thankfully, we always had adequate basements to store our seasonal clothing by size to go from one boy to the next. What was extra cool was my two sisters and two of Michael's sisters only had one boy each (in addition to girls) and generously passed on their son's clothing to us – like brand new!!! Gary Hawes used to teach on how God can stretch out a budget that is committed to Him. We tried to live out Gary's words of, "Wear it out, make it do, use it up, go without." We never went without. In fact, there would be times one of the boys would need a new winter jacket because they had outgrown the previous one. God knew that, but He wanted us to ask Him and to recognize He was the Provider. Sometimes I would forget to ask and would just layer the guys up for warmth. Sure enough, as soon as I would pray, a box would arrive in the mail from a sister or friend with just what we needed. It was rare for us to ever buy anything but underwear and shoes. The boys would be told what we would spend on shoes and if they wanted "better," it would come out of their allowance. We would always pray before going shopping for great deals on what we needed. They became great shoppers and prayer warriors! It was fun to watch God provide their dream shoes ON SALE! Great laughter occurs when the boys look at old pictures and say, "MOM, I can't believe you made me wear that!" Can you believe they survived?

And, yes, because we thought we were done having children, Matt was a little spoiled as he was blessed with a new wardrobe when he came along. However, he is in Florida now wearing some of Dan and John's clothes because he did not pack enough of the right kind of business clothes for the summer working with Danny.

I, too, would hold onto clothes for my many "seasons" of life, much to my sister Patti's chagrin. In trying to follow Gary's sagely advice, I had skinny clothes, not so thin clothes, holiday clothes, fat clothes, maternity clothes, and back to skinny clothes just in time to get pregnant again...and again...and again...and again. Now that I have "matured," I just have everyday clothes, of course, for every season. A great blessing is passing on clothes to others. I know I have far more clothes than I truly need. To curb my shopping, I will not allow myself to buy something unless I give something away. It is amazing how it makes me think before I buy because I like what I have and I know IF I buy one outfit, one outfit has to go. If I buy two things, two things have to go, etcetera.

One of our most favorite games to play as we traveled as a family was to pretend what we would do if we were given a million dollars. As the boys grew, we saw their hearts grow too. Instead of buying expensive cars or going on fancy trips, they started giving it away to this person or that ministry. Best of all, they are living it out today; not with a million dollars but with hearts worth MUCH MORE!

Madeline Holben, the 91 year old mother of my dear friend, Sue Holben, recently died. The church was packed with friends and relatives to honor this wonderful woman. It was fun to hear all of the marvelous ways Madeline touched her children, grandchildren and friends. I LOVE the example of a GIVING life Madeline lived out and the legacy she left her children and grandchildren. When Sue's son, Michael, moved into his own apartment, Grandma Madeline left the following directions on 'How to Live a Life Well' hanging in one of his kitchen cupboards:

Live your life as an exclamation, not an explanation.
Cherish your children for what they are, not for what you want them to be.
Never waste an opportunity to tell someone you love them.
Be forgiving of yourself and others.
Watch a sunrise at least once a year.
Be there when people need you.
Always accept an outstretched hand.
Show respect for all living things.
Carry jumper cables in your trunk. ☺
Become the most positive and enthusiastic person you know.
Strive for excellence, not perfection.
Keep your promises.
Count your blessings!
TRUST GOD!

We know the things of this world will pass away. What we leave in Jesus' Name will never pass away. Instead of living extravagantly, we choose to invest in eternally significant things, like sending souls to Heaven! I do not know how many times we have thought about doing "this or that" just when a Kingdom opportunity comes along. It might be to support a missionary, a matching gift to send Bibles to soldiers, food to a country in the name of Christ, or…an endless list of far more worthy needs than a "this or a that." Now when money is comes from something unexpected, or expected, like a tax return, we start praying about where we can send our tithe. What a privilege and marvelous blessing to freely give as we have been freely given to by our Jehovah Jireh!

Casting Crowns sings a marvelous song about how the Body of Christ needs to be living and working together as God intended in **"If We Are The Body."** As God's Body, we need to be reaching with our arms, healing with our hands, teaching with our words, going with our feet to show the world JESUS!

Is it not time for us to start honoring and obeying our Jehovah Jireh? God has **SO MUCH MORE** for us when we listen and obey. Praise Him!

CHAPTER 26

ENLARGE OUR TERRITORY

The Prayer of Jabez:
"Jabez cried out to the God of Israel,
'Oh, that you would bless me and enlarge my territory!
Let Your hand be with me, and keep me from
harm so that I will be free from pain.'
And God granted his request."
I Chronicles 4:10

I realize it now! The day I began praying this prayer is the day my boys started looking to new horizons. **Oh my!** It is all my fault that every one of our five boys have moved away and 4 out of 5 live out of state! That will teach me to take God seriously!!!

It was in February of 2001 that I was first introduced to the **Prayer of Jabez by Bruce Wilkinson**. Since then, I have prayed it almost everyday. I was so impressed by the book and its concept that I went out and bought 30 copies to pass out to whomever God laid on my heart. Of course, Michael read it and also was touched. We gave it to our three older boys. Steve was so challenged by it he went out and bought more for himself to hand out, including one for my sister, Kaye (Leslie – they share the same middle name after my Dad), and also one for Carl Seestedt, who was the father of one of his best friends, Julie. It so touched Carl that he told Steve and us that because of Steve giving him that book, he wanted to reconnect with God. Carl and his wife, Vicki, started coming to our church, which was a delight! The very next year, Carl found out he had a brain tumor that took him and his family down a long, difficult road, but with an amazing attitude and twinkle in his eye. In June of 2009, Carl reconnected with God in Heaven. His funeral was a beautiful testimony of God's and Carl's mutual love for one another. I recognize that story could make you NOT want to pray the prayer. But Carl was going to die anyway; God used that book and His Word to make sure he was ready.

As I gaze upon one of our family pictures, my personalized prayer goes something like this: Thank You, Lord, for blessing us mightily. I pray that You continue to bless us indeed. Enlarge our territory, that Your hand would be with us. Keep us from evil and evil from us that we might not cause pain, that we might not sin against You. In Jesus Name, Amen.

I would like to tell you it works and is the most wonderful thing EVER! Sorry. It does "work" because God answers prayer, but we have gone through some really rough times since that first prayer. However, I take great comfort in knowing God has been with us through it all. "That **YOUR hand would be with us**" is my favorite part of the prayer and has become my focus. To know the hand of GOD is with you is an immeasurable joy!

David Wilkinson explains the prayer beautifully and I encourage you to get the book for yourself. I shall touch upon his thoughts, but mainly, "So why not ask?" God tells us to ask and claim His many promises. Moses asked God to "Show me Your glory" (Exodus 33:18). "God's bounty is limited only by us, not by His resources, power, or willingness to give... God's nature is to bless" (page 29). "The reason some men and women of faith rise above the rest is they think and pray differently than those around them" (page 19). "The Jabez blessing focuses like a laser on our wanting for ourselves nothing more and nothing less than what God wants for us" (page 24). Back to that immeasurable joy. God knows it is not the mountaintops but the valleys we go through that make us more Christ like.

I see enlarging our territories as spreading out our boundaries for outreach. Wilkinson says on page 30, it is "So that you can make a greater impact for Him," **making ourselves available to have HIM do more through us**. We are reminded in Zechariah 4:6, "Not by might nor by power but by MY SPIRIT says the Lord." God always desires us to remember life **IS** all about Him and His glory, not our own. "If you are doing your business (LIFE) God's way, it's not only right to ask for more, but He is waiting for you to ask. Your business (life) is the territory God has entrusted to you. He wants you to accept it as a significant opportunity to touch individual lives, the business community, and the larger world for His glory. Asking Him to enlarge that opportunity brings Him only delight" (pages 30 & 31). **I want to see Jesus smile with delight!!!**

"To pray for larger borders is to ask for a miracle – it's that simple. A miracle is an intervention by God to make something happen that wouldn't normally happen" (page 43). Do you believe in miracles? I do! If God desires to do something supernaturally, would you object? Why are we afraid of things we do not understand? God tells us to fear HIM and be filled with awe! Forget putting Him in a box that you can explain. If you do, then He would not be God. I do not want a God I can totally explain. I want a God Who is **MUCH MORE** than I could ever hope or imagine (Ephesians 3:20). "Oh, the depth of the riches of the wisdom and knowledge of God! How unsearchable His judgments, and His paths beyond tracing out! Who has known the mind of the Lord? Or who has been His counselor? Who has ever given to God, that God should repay him? **For from Him and through Him and to Him are ALL things. To Him be the glory forever" (Romans 11:33 – 36)!**

Michael and I were so challenged by this book that we gave one to each of our elders at West Lansing Church of Christ. We asked them to pray and consider how we could enlarge our territory for Christ in our community. We were a praying

church but I really felt God wanted us to enlist the prayer warriors of our church to pray specifically for the worship service
and each member by name during the worship service every
week. The elders agreed and asked me if I would be willing to
oversee this ministry…I was elated!!! So I prayed and asked
God to show me who HE wanted to be a part of this team. He
clearly showed me He wanted our elders and their wives to
participate. They each agreed readily. Then God asked me to
go to specific members in the congregation, give them one of
the books, and ask them to read it and pray about being on
the team.

Of course this whole process took a couple of months,
which seemed like eternity to me. God reminded me His
time is always perfect, never rushed. Argh! It just seems like
MUCH MORE could be done for the Kingdom if people would
just move a whole lot faster! He agreed, more could get done
BUT He wanted it done right, HIS WAY! Once again, no surprise, He was right! There were a few people asked who said
no. That was okay. God even showed me whom He wanted
paired with whom. Obviously, married couples with each other.
Women with women. Men with men. We called our group the
Jabez Prayer Group. There were 26 of us and with 52 weeks
in a year, we met by two's to pray in Michael's office during
the service about every 13 weeks; not a hardship on any of
us to miss 4 services a year. Instead, we each saw it as a
real honor to lift up the congregation before our Lord for His
blessing upon our lives as He enlarged our territory for His
glory. We saw countless things happen because GOD worked
through the prayers of His people. God always blesses and
sends the people and/or resources needed when you put His
agenda ahead of your own. At the very least, which is MUCH,
our prayer life increased. I know God was smiling!

This ministry has continued at West Lansing Church of
Christ. Much to our surprise, we were taken out of it when
God decided to move us elsewhere, enlarging our territory
and that of the church. We praise Him! We have always told
God however and wherever He needs to use us, we are avail-

able. Again, He has taken us seriously because we have taken Him seriously. I confess it has not always been my timing nor choice of location but I have always felt His hand leading, even when I was surrounded by clouds and could not see Him. Sometimes we do not even "feel" very useful but God tells us to trust Him, not our feelings. He just wants us to make ourselves available for Him to use, to be open vessels for His Spirit to flow through freely. He also reminds me everything is about HIS glory, not mine. Another favorite book of mine that goes along with this concept is **If You Want To Walk On Water, You've Got To Get Out Of The Boat** by **John Ortberg**. It is all about us saying YES to Jesus! Ortberg says, "Your boat is whatever represents safety and security to you apart from God Himself" (page 17). The book challenges us to put our trust in God alone and to watch Him work His miracles in and through us.

God wants to work with, in, and through us. He is seeking loyal followers who sincerely look for His hand to be the power and presence in their lives. When you step out with God, you need not have fear. II Chronicles 16:9 says, "For the eyes of the Lord runs to and fro throughout the whole earth, to show Himself strong on behalf of those whose heart is loyal to Him." Dependence on God is not a weakness but is His strength in us. **God is mighty to save!**

In praying for God to keep us from evil and evil from us, the best offense is the strongest defense; stay away from it! God talks about "Your ENEMY, the devil, prowls around like a roaring lion looking for someone to devour" (I Peter 5:8). Wilkinson declares, "By far our most important strategy for defeating the roaring lion is to stay out of the arena" (page 63). **DO NOT OPEN THE DOOR OF TEMPTATION. YOU WILL BE DEVOURED!** Instead, IF you do not know, ask God to show you what your weaknesses are and stay FAR away from them. It is much easier and far wiser to avoid temptations than to think we are super Christians and will not be affected. That is called pride and stupidity. I know too many "strong" Christians who have been devoured because they were depending on themselves to beat temptation away rather than obeying God and staying clear of it. Too often it is the "strong" Christian who causes the most pain, leaders who have opened and stepped through the door of temptation. We are not in a bubble and our actions do affect others. Life will cause pain. Christians will sin. I believe when we who profess to be lovers of Jesus CHOOSE to stray from the path of righteousness, it is detrimental to the Kingdom. Not only does it affect our relationship with God, but it hurts our family, friends, and all who know us; including our influence upon potential future believers. We now have become a hindrance – heaven forbid! Can God bring good out of bad? Absolutely! But only He knows the long range effect of sin on the lives of others. It is far better to avoid it and the pain that comes with sin, letting our lives bring glory to His name, not darkness.

"Hear Us From Heaven," by Jared Anderson, is a song of prayer. We Christians need to cry out in desperation for the healing of our land. Let us ask God to hear us, dwell in us, and use us to touch our generation. May we TOGETHER intentionally live to enlarge HIS territory so that those around us may see, hear, and come to know the love of God.

Will we ask and expect God to make us a blessing to the countless people in our world who need His touch through us? We are His plan for saving the world. He needs US to show them Jesus! God knows that His Spirit flowing through us is MUCH MORE powerful in attracting others to the Kingdom. People need God, but want someone with skin on. **WE are His MUCH MORE!**

CHAPTER 27

FIRST OF ALL,
PRAY, PRAY, PRAY, and PRAY!!!!

*"I urge then, first of all, that requests, prayers,
intercessions and thanksgiving be made for everyone…"*
I Timothy 2:1

Once upon a time, years and years ago, in a land far away (Brighton, Michigan), Dave McFaddin spoke on the above verse and beautifully pointed out the priority God puts on prayer – to do it! Not only does God call us to pray, but in case we miss it the first time, He tells us three more times. God wants us to get hold of Him. God wants to get hold of us!

Books and books have been written on prayer. This little chapter is not meant to be a treatise on prayer. It is simply a reminder of how MUCH God wants us to know Him, how He calls us to Himself, and allows us to be a part of touching the world for Him. God is our goal in prayer.

Pray for everyone! EVERYONE? Wow! That is a big order! God has a big love that reaches out to the whole world… **everyone!** I Timothy 2:2–6 & 8 say "For kings and all those in authority, that we may live peaceful and quiet lives in all godliness and holiness. This is good, and pleases God our Savior, Who wants ALL men (women) to be saved and to come to a knowledge of the Truth. For there is one God and one mediator between God and men, the man Christ Jesus, Who gave Himself as a ransom for ALL men (women)...I want men (women) EVERYWHERE to lift up holy hands in prayer, WITHOUT anger or disputing."

I think sometimes we stop short of God's best because we are overwhelmed and think we cannot do it all. We cannot. **That is why we have Jesus!** We see 'Pray for EVERYONE' and think we could not even get through all the people in Michigan before the next day and yet God wants us to pray for everyone? There is more to life than just praying! Right again, like getting to know the ones God has placed around us. Why not start praying for them? It is my "secret" to learning the names of those God places in my life.

'For kings and ALL those in authority'??? Again, another big order. Break it down. Pray for our "king," our president. I confess I did not vote for President Obama and I do not agree with much of anything that he is doing, but he IS our president and I will pray for him daily. I know God loves our leaders, and, for whatever reason, has placed them in authority. My job is to pray. I trust GOD to work in and through the person and position. I also pray for our President's staff, cabinet, Supreme Court Justices, national branches of government, our state government, county, city, and local fire and police... and their families. I even ask God to remind me whenever I see American flags flying to pray for our government, those in authority, and our military.

Again, too much? Ask God for whom He would have you pray. You already know 'those in authority.' How about church leaders? Fathers? Mothers? Employers? Teachers? Ask God to foil the plans of the enemy so that those you are praying for will come to a knowledge of the Truth, the Good News of Jesus. God so wants us to know Him. He wants us to come free from the destruction of anger within ourselves and from disputations with others. He desires us to be one with Him. When we release our anger it removes barriers that we have allowed to come between us and God. This freedom empowers God to work in and through us. What an honor, what a privilege.

Too many times we come to prayer as a function to cross off our list of things to do. Instead, we need to come to Jesus. There is a beautiful song out right now called **"What Do I Know Of Holy?" by Addison Road**. God wants us to know Holy. He wants us to know Him. That is why He calls us to prayer. <u>**God Calling**</u> asks, "Have you ever realized the wonder of the friendship you can have with Me? Have you ever thought what it means to be able to summon at will the God of the World? Even with a privileged visitor to an earthly king there is the palace antechamber, and the time must be at the pleasure of the king. But to My subjects I have given the right to enter My Presence when they will, nay more, they can summon Me to bedside, to workshop – and I am there" (June 25).

Again, prayer is about getting to know the God of prayer, NOT about getting the answers. In I Timothy 2:1, God mentions the following four types of prayers, starting with the one most of us exclusively use for prayer:

REQUESTS – are simply coming before the King of the Universe and laying out your wants and needs, whatever they are. (The very fact that I can use "simply" and "King" in the same sentence reminds me of the great wonder of prayer.)

PRAYERS – are sharing your thoughts and wonderings, more of a dialogue.

INTERCESSION - is work. Ozzie says, "Intercession means raising ourselves up to the point of getting the mind of Christ regarding the person for whom we are praying" (March 30). "In the life of a saint there is no such thing as chance…God brings you to places, among people, and into certain conditions to accomplish a definite purpose through the intercession of the Spirit in you. Your part in intercessory prayer is not to agonize over how to intercede, but to use the everyday circumstances and people God puts around you by His providence to bring them before His throne, and to allow the Spirit in you the opportunity to intercede for them. Without the intercession, the lives of others would be left in poverty and in ruin" (November 7). "True intercession involves bringing the person, or the circumstance that seems to be crashing in on you, before God, until you are changed by His attitude toward that person or circumstance. **Intercession is putting yourself in God's place; it is having His mind and His perspective. Intercession is the only thing that has no drawbacks, because it keeps our relationship completely open with God.** What we must avoid in intercession is praying for someone to be simply 'patched up.' We must pray that person completely through into contact with the very life of God" (December 13). Contact with us is just contact. Contact with God is life. This is why we pray, to connect others with God, allowing His life to pour into and through our lives to others.

THANKSGIVING - is recognizing from Whom all things come and thanking Him, counting our innumerable blessings. **There is such a joy in thanksgiving as you look around, knowing in the very depths of your heart all is okay because God remains on His throne.** Even this pain or that urgency has not shaken His grip on life. It has not come upon Him by surprise. I rest in God being in charge because I trust Him. He has proven Himself over and over. **I choose** to remember His hand in my life. I do not fear tomorrow because He is already there.

An excellent book by our dear friend, **Dean Trune,** is **The Path Toward Passion**. In it Dean shares nine disciplines that connect your heart to God's. Dean travels the world with Intentional Impact Ministries teaching how to prepare and order your life for God's dwelling so that we impact the world for Him. **God's intent for us is to first pray, pray, pray, and pray so that we will intimately come to know the Creator of the Universe, being His MUCH MORE!!!**

CHAPTER 28

EVERYTHING WE NEED

"His divine power has given us
EVERYTHING WE NEED for life and godliness
through our knowledge of Him
Who called us by His own glory and goodness."
I Peter 1:3

When I ran across this verse years ago I stopped dead in my tracks. Not only did the very statement boggle my mind, but it confused me. If God has given us <u>everything</u> we need, why do <u>I</u> want so much? Why do <u>I</u> "feel" so ineffective? I think it comes back to focus. Is my life centered around God, or centered around me? Where is my focus? Am I going to believe my feelings, or God's Word? Receive and Believe; receiving His promises and teachings, I choose to believe.

In I Peter, God tells us He wants us to <u>participate</u> in His divine nature (verse 4) and to add to our faith goodness, knowledge, self-control, perseverance, godliness, brotherly kindness, and love (verses 5–7). He continues to instruct us with the promise that as these qualities grow in increasing measure, we will be effective, productive, and never fall (verse 10). Best of all, "We shall receive a rich welcome into the eternal kingdom of our Lord and Savior Jesus Christ" (verse

11). What else do we need besides a rich welcome into the Kingdom?!!!

My problem is I want it all NOW. I am lazy and do not want to have to work. After all, I am a daughter of the KING, am I not entitled to all that He owns? Absolutely, but riches come with responsibility. Growing up my parents gave us kids a weekly allowance. It was an agreement we made. IF we did the jobs given to us, they would pay us an allowance. It did not take me long to realize that IF I did not do my job, I did not receive an allowance. Same too with God...if I do not follow His guidelines, will I receive my reward. Should I?

Years ago when Michael and I were newly married, we were each in a small discipleship group with Gary Hawes, our minister and friend. I was with women, Michael was with men. Gary challenged us to choose a life verse that we felt God was directing us to and one that came alive for us. Recognizing the relationship I was entering into with the Lordship of Christ, I noticed more and more IF/THEN verses. Salvation is free, Lordship is conditional. I chose Psalms 84:11. My paraphrased version is, "The Lord is my sun and my shield. He will give me grace and glory and no good thing will He withhold from me IF I walk uprightly." Although I have failed many times to walk uprightly, God has never failed. I cling to that promise.

How many kids entering kindergarten graduate the next year from high school? None, it is a process. I do not know how many times I panicked thinking there was NO WAY I was going to ever understand the math Kaye and Scott were doing. It is a process. A foundation is laid and built upon so that we are prepared to receive the new material. First we learn the alphabet, then letters become words, words become sentences, sentences become paragraphs and so it goes. The same thing happens with numbers. First we learn to count, then these numbers take on meaning and we learn to combine them. It is a process. Children cannot learn geography until they have learned about the safety of their home and neighborhood. It is a process. How many college graduates receive jobs requiring five years experience right out of college? It is a process. We humans want to skip the work and get to the top, instantaneously. Too many newlyweds buy a house and want to fill it with furniture forgetting that it took their parents years and years to work and save for the house in which they live. We are spoiled by instant gratification – and we all know how healthy fast food is – things that are worthwhile take time (except maybe McDonald's french fries).

Back to the basics. A firm foundation needs to be laid in a new Christian's life too. It would be wrong for us who have been Christians longer to expect a new Christian to be living a perfect life. We do not even do it! But we can and should be striving to live like Jesus everyday. The fundamentals need to be shown and taught by us so that they can be caught and practiced by the babe in Christ. God knows we are slow to learn. In Hebrews 5:12-14, He tells us, "Though by this time you ought to be teachers, you need someone to teach you the elementary truths of God's Word all over again. You need milk, not solid food! Anyone who lives on milk, being still an infant, is not acquainted with the teaching about righteousness. But solid food is for the mature, who by <u>constant use</u> have <u>trained</u> themselves to distinguish good from evil." Not only would we never expect an adult to survive and thrive on just milk, we would expect a baby to choke on meat. Spiritual growth is also a process of being <u>trained</u> by hearing and seeing the Word in action by other Christians and then by <u>constant use</u> in our own lives, day by day. God is far more patient with us than we are with ourselves and each other. We all want grace, but often refuse to give it. Life and Christianity is a process that takes time. The best solution is to listen to the One Who created both life and time.

As we near the end of this book, I feel like Peter. I want to ask questions of those to whom I am writing and remind you of things GOD wants you to remember. Are the truths we know in our head, being lived out in our heart? Are they real to us? If they are, do others around us know it by our actions? I have heard an analogy that some people miss Heaven by 18" – the distance between the head and the heart. Knowledge without application is useless. Just like the Dead Sea, input without output leads to stagnation; the stench of being filled up with yourself. How many more Bible Studies and Christian conferences do we need to go to before we put the information to use by sharing it with others? How many Christians say they want to be missionaries, but have never even talked to their neighbor or coworker? Shame on us! Why do we think we can be used of God elsewhere when we are not allowing Him to use us where we are now? God does not give us the Bible to make us smarter but to change our lives, AND the lives of those around us!

God IS everything we need. Without Christ, everything else is empty. I have been told by some people that they feel like they are a project to me. I tell them they are half right. Although I never intend for them to feel anything BUT loved, I do purpose to introduce them to Jesus. That is my goal for everyone I meet. I want them to meet and grow in Christ. After all, if they just get to know me, our friendship dies when I do. But if they get to know Jesus, our friendship goes on forever; and so do they!!! The greatest love I can give anyone is Jesus – **HE IS LIFE!** If I say I believe in Jesus and life ever after, am I loving you if I do not share Jesus and challenge you with His best? I see it as my duty, my very reason for living. Why else does God bring you into my life? So if you have felt like a project with me, I am sorry. I see our time together as me giving you the **ultimate gift – JESUS!** Yes, time together is precious and relationships grow that way, but life is too short and there are too many people dying and going to Hell. Chit chat is fine for some, and I am quite good at small talk myself, but it is called "small talk" for a reason – it has no purpose except to fill time. We have too little time to waste. I confess there have been a few people I have met with whom I did not want to share Jesus because I did not want to spend eternity with them. Shame on me! That is called judgment, selfishness, and sin! I have had to cry out for God's forgiveness as He died for their souls too. We are to love as He loves. WE all need JESUS!!! Peter says, "I think it is right to refresh your memory as long as I live in the tent of this body...I will make every effort to see that after my departure you will always be able to REMEMBER these things" (I Peter 1: 13–15). Not my words, God's Word.

It is funny to me how the 23rd Psalm seems to be a comfort to many and is said often by rote at funerals, whether the deceased or family of the deceased knows the Shepherd or not. Verse one jumped out at me several funerals ago, "The Lord is my Shepherd, I shall not want." Translated, I need nothing. The New Living Translation actually says, "**The Lord is my Shepherd; I have EVERYTHING I need.**" Do I believe that? I say I do, especially when I am getting everything I want. But what about the times I THINK I have a void in my life? How real is it to me then? Truly, a shepherd's very role, his "job description," is to care for all the needs of his sheep. So, IF I look to my Savior, my Lord, as my Shepherd, do I trust Him to provide all of my needs? I am choosing to believe not only that **God can** but that **He does and will provide everything I need**. If I do not get something, it must not be a need.

Same thing with Proverbs 37:4, "Delight yourself in the Lord and He will give you the desires of your heart." So many have said to me they delighted themselves with Jesus, but never got what they wanted. I question that. IF Jesus is your focus and you are delighting in Him, surrounded with His glory, what else could you want?!!! Yes, I have wanted much, but in my seeking the face and heart of my Lord those wants have paled in significance, if not totally vanished. My heart has often been redirected, being freed from some things that could have caused bondage. How can Jesus not be enough?

A basic thing in life is vocations and occupations. I have come to understand that my calling in life, my vocation, is to bring glory to God in all I do. My occupation, my job, can change by education to market availability to economy downswings or upswings. **My vocation remains the same; to bring glory to God**. So, no matter what job I have, or do not have, God is still to be glorified. God never intended us to struggle with some things, yet we do. We need to surrender it all to Him and trust Him. Period. He can use us wherever our occupation takes us or leaves us. I choose to believe God is in charge of my life. IF I am living His Will for my life, I also believe it is God Who gives to me and allows things to be taken away. It is not some employer, some spouse, some parent/child, or any "body" responsible for my life. I do not blame anyone nor empower them to have control over my feelings. I **choose to trust God** and give Him the credit, expecting Him to bring glory to His name through every good and seemingly bad thing that happens in my life. He never wastes pain. Max Lucado says, "When you can't trace God's hand, trust His heart."

Gary Chapman in **The Five Love Languages** says, "I am amazed by how many individuals mess up every new day with yesterday…they bring in failures of yesterday…and pollute a potentially wonderful day" (page 46). God intends for our yesterdays to help redirect our todays so that we can confidently walk into our tomorrows, knowing He is already there waiting for us. Jesus says, "I am going to prepare a place for you" (John 14: 2). He wants our eyes on Him, looking for His hand, trusting His heart. **He IS everything we need!**

Talk about a career shift. You all know by now that I am a Mom of five incredible sons. Although I will always be their Mom, my input in their life is different, as it is supposed to be. Two years ago when our youngest, Matt, went off to college my "occupation" changed but my "vocation" remained the same, to bring glory to God. Much of this change is fun as Michael and I explore new areas of adventure with our "extra" time. No longer do I have seven mouths to feed, nor laundry to do for five active boys, now men. Believe it or not, I terribly miss my job as Mom. I miss having them in and out of the house with friends, playing together, just sitting and talking over meals, and worshiping together. I also recognize that specific "occupation" was for a season, and rather than cry because it is over, I smile because it has happened.

The three rules of real estate is location, location, location. In Christianity, Ozzie says "Your priorities must be God 1st, God 2nd, God 3rd, until your life is continually face to face with

God and no one else is taken into account whatsoever" (July 13). This world of ours has many things to offer. With those offers, we can get confused and be led astray. One of the most helpful things for me when I feel confused is to go back to the basics, that **JESUS LOVES ME!** Yes, I even sometimes sing my favorite song, "Jesus Loves Me, this I know, for the Bible tells me so." **I KNOW, because I CHOOSE to believe what God tells me in the Bible.** It does not say because I "feel," but because I "know" – my head and my heart connect. **I am His and He is mine. He is EVERYTHING I need.** Period. I tune out the world and all of its voices. I choose to let Jesus sing to me, minister to me, provide what I need... **EVERYTHING** that I need. Is Jesus enough for you?

CAUTION: If Jesus is not enough, nothing will ever be enough. Look into His face and see His smile and hear His heart beat for YOU! JESUS is EVERYTHING we need and SO MUCH MORE!!!

CHAPTER 29

PREDESTINED FOR HIS GLORY!!!

"Christ in you, the hope of glory." Colossians 1:27
"The Word became flesh…we have seen
His glory." John 1:14
"Now, show me Your glory". Exodus 33:18

So now what? Are we anymore aware that **WE are God's MUCH MORE**? Do we believe **He is everything we need**, the **Lover of our soul**? Are we ready to say, Lord, show me Your glory? There is a song by **Hillsong United Live** called <u>**You Are Here**</u> which reminds me of God's power in us and desire for us. As Christians, we have the Holy Spirit living within us. Therefore, the **SAME** sacrificial love that sent Jesus to save me and the miraculous power that raised Him from the dead lives in me, lives in you! What are we going to do with that thought? God gives us choices, but His hope and plan for us is to open ourselves up to Him so that He may live through us to touch lives for Him. We cannot do it on our own. We need to be filled with His grace and Truth. It is not about us. **It is all about Him and for His glory! God's Holy Spirit in me, our Hope of glory!**

How? I do not know. It is another God "thing" that boggles my mind. Simply put, God knows and we do not have to. It is His business. He said it so I believe it! Another family analogy that helps me understand an inkling of all of this is our five sons have a part of us living in them…and I do know how that all happened. ☺ Genetically, they have some of both Michael and me. They have been taught, and therefore caught, much of what makes us who we are. They have learned the passions of our hearts. Each son, in their own way and time, has taken ownership of some or much of those thoughts and beliefs; some have been disregarded. Choices. A heritage has been passed down to them and they have the freewill to carry on what they believe is best. I, too, have the freewill to choose what God has passed on to me – whether to receive and believe it or to disregard. For our sons to disregard some of our teachings may not be detrimental. For me to disregard God's teaching will be MUCH MORE than detrimental. Consequences will incur, but I still have the choice whether to have Christ living in me or not. So do you.

God has proven Himself over and over to me. He has shown me His path and I have followed, not always liking the view. But who am I to question my Creator? He did not ask me if I wanted to be born – He chose LIFE for me! Predestined? Yes, in the sense that God chose to give me breath with the hopes we would live for HIS glory. Besides that, we are NOT puppets. He shows us the way, His way, and allows us freedom to pull our own strings. All things in this world are not good; there are ugly things. But we know God can work IN all things for good. Romans 8:28 & 29 says, "We know that in all things, God works together for good, for those who are called according to His purpose. For those God foreknew (hello! like everybody!), He also predestined <u>to be conformed to the likeness of His Son</u>." God wants us to walk, talk and look like Jesus…**ALL for HIS glory!** Do people see Jesus in us?

Though some will say God predestined only a select few to be saved, I believe Scripture teaches us that He predestined ALL to be saved; but WE choose otherwise. The offer remains on "the table." We have to be careful not to buy into the divisive issues Satan so wants to use on Christians. Just as with parenting, ask yourself if this is the hill you want to die on… is it crucial unto salvation? This is where I put earplugs in so I can only hear God speaking to me. I put blinders on so that I can only see, through His Word, what HE is saying to me. We are born into families who show us their ways; some good, some not. As we grow, it is vitally important that we recognize the good intentions of family, friends, church, and other influencers to teach us what they know. Sometimes what they know is NOT Truth. We must go to the Source of Truth and see for ourselves what God desires, yes, even intends, for our lives. Michael and I have always encouraged those we have known to NOT take our word as gospel, but to go to the Source of the Gospel themselves. Verify truths or disarm lies (some intentional, most are misunderstandings) spoken to you by confirming it with God's Word. This I know: God has predestined us for HIS glory!

For awhile the Jewish nation was God's favored people, but when they turned their back on Him, He chose to send a Savior for ALL people. John 3:16 & 17 is clear when it says that "God so loved THE WORLD that He gave His one and only Son, that WHOEVER believes in Him shall not perish but have eternal life. For God did not send His Son into the world to condemn the world, but TO SAVE THE WORLD through Him." Many, many other verses support God's love for everyone, but John 1:11 & 12 ties this all together with "He came to that which was His own (Jews) but His own did not receive Him. Yet to ALL who received Him, to those who believed in His name, He gave the right to become children of God." Precious rights. WE choose whether we accept God as our Father. He has already chosen us to be His child, **His MUCH MORE**. He will not make us, He allows us to choose. Yes, it is God's desire, His will for us to choose Him. God has pre-destined us for His best…life with Him forever! Our destiny is held in His nail-pierced hands. We decide. Who or what will we place on the throne of our lives? God holds out to us His Hope of Glory, Jesus. Will we receive Him? We decide.

God's hope is not only that we receive Christ, but that we choose to honor Him with every fiber of our body. In doing so, we bring Him glory. With God's grace, our very lives will point to Jesus! I Thessalonians 1:12 says, "By His power He may fulfill every good purpose of yours and every act prompted by your faith…so that the name of our Lord Jesus may be glorified in you, and you in Him, according to the grace of our God and the Lord Jesus Christ." God is glorified by our praise (Psalm 22:23), good works (Matthew 5:16), fruit (John 15:8), spiritual unity (Romans 15:6), and our being sold out for Jesus! Not only have we been given life, a life has been given for us. We have been bought with a price (I Corinthians 6:20). **I choose to give back my life to the Giver of Life, for His glory.** I choose to consecrate my entire life and body to honor Him. **WE ARE HIS MUCH MORE!** When will we begin living like it?

Another beautiful song by Third Day is "Show Me Your Glory." It magnifies the glory of the Lord in everything around us. Once we open our eyes and see God in His majesty, we never want to let go, we never want to settle for anything but His face, His glory, His life amidst and through our life!

God has not brought us this far to leave us hanging. Open your eyes and see His glory all around you. See Him winking at you in the stars. Listen to God singing His love songs to you through the birds chirping or in a child's laughter. Feel His arms of love wrapped securely around you through the breezes pushing or pulling you along your journey. Taste and see that He is good. Things may not be good, but **God IS good, all the time. All the time, God IS good!** Believe it and see it!

As God cares for the birds of the air, **SO MUCH MORE** He cares for us. He says it, I believe it! Birds are care free. They come expecting to be watered and fed, singing along their way. I, too, want to come to my Father, expecting to be watered and fed…singing His praises! Wanna join me?

WE are the MUCH MORE!!!

BIBLIOGRAPHY

Bailey, Ney. <u>Faith Is Not a Feeling</u>. Here's Life Publishers, San Bernardino, CA, 1978.

Birkey, Verna. <u>God's Pattern for Contentment and Peace...In a Stressful World</u>. Enriched Living Workshops, Kent, WA, 1986.

Bridges, Jerry. <u>The Pursuit of Holiness</u>. NavPress, Colorado Springs, CO, 2006.

Chambers, Oswald. <u>MY UTMOST FOR HIS HIGHEST</u>. Discovery House Publishers, Grand Rapids, MI, 1992.

Chapman, Gary. <u>The Five Love Languages</u>. Northfield Publishing, Chicago, IL, 1995.

Dobson, James. <u>The Strong Willed Child, Birth Through Adolescence</u>. Tyndale House Publishers, Wheaton, IL, 2004, Chapter 9.

Eggerich, Emerson and Sarah. <u>Love and Respect</u>. Love and Respect Ministries, Grand Rapids, MI, 2006.

Evans, Colleen Townsend. <u>The Vine Life</u>. Chosen Books, Lincoln, VA, 1980.

Farrel, Bill and Pam. <u>Men Are Like Waffles, Women Are Like Spaghetti</u>. Harvest House Publishers, Eugene, OR, 2001.

Howe, Desiree Lyon. <u>Porphyria, A Lyon's Share of Trouble</u>. Digital Datawerks, Los Angelos, CA, 2004.

Lucado, Max. <u>Fearless</u>. Thomas Nelson, Nashville, TN, 2009.

Mains, David and Karen. <u>Tales of the Kingdom</u>. Lamplighter Publisher, Waverly, PA, 1983.

—. <u>Tales of the Resistance</u>. Lamplighter Publisher, Waverly, PA, 1986.

—. <u>Tales of the Restoration</u>. Lamplighter Publisher, Waverly, PA, 1996.

"Multi-Infarct Dementia." <u>Mayo Clinic Family Health Book</u>. William Morrow, New York, NY, 1990, 518.

Ortberg, John. <u>If You Want To Walk On Water, You've Got To Get Out Of The Boat</u>. Zondervan, Grand Rapids, MI, 2001

<u>Our Daily Bread</u>. RBC Ministries, Grand Rapids, MI, March – May, 2010.

Piper, John. <u>Don't Waste Your Life</u>. Crossway Books, A Division of Good News Publishers, Wheaton, IL, 2003.

Russell, A. J. <u>God Calling</u>. Barbour, Uhrichsville, OH, 1953.

Spranger, Kim. <u>Riding God's Rainbow</u>. 2004 (unpublished).

Swindoll, Charles. <u>Living Above the Level of Mediocrity: A Commitment to Excellence</u>. Word Books Publisher, Waco, TX, 1987.

Trune, Dean. <u>The PathToward Passion, Nine Disciplines that Connect Your Heart to God's</u>. PrayerShop Publishing, Terre Haute, IN, 2009.

Wilkenson, Bruce. <u>The Prayer of Jabez, Breaking Through to the Blessed Life</u>. Multnomah Publishers, Sisters, OR, 2000.

SONGS MENTIONED

Chapter 5:   "Be Thou My Vision," Eleanor Hull, Public Domain, 1912.
"Fill Me Up," Don Poythress and Jared Anderson, Integrity, 2009.

Chapter 7:   "Constant Companion," Bob Fitts, Integrity, 2002.

Chapter 9:   "Expectation," Don Poythress and Tony Wood, Integrity, 2009.

Chapter 12:   "Power of Your Love," Hillsong, Integrity, 1998.

Chapter 13:   "Count Your Blessings," Johnson Oatman, Jr., Public Domain, 1897.
"Jesus, Lover of My Soul," Hillsong, Integrity, 1992.

Chapter 14:   "Doxology," Thomas Ken, Public Domain, 1674.
"Satisfy," 10th Avenue North, 2008.
"Victory In Jesus," Eugene Monroe Bartlett, Public Domain, 1939.

Chapter 16:   "Go Light Your World," Chris Rice, 2004.

"Top of My Lungs," Craig and Dean Phillips, 2006.

Chapter 18:   "The Stand," Hillsong United, 2006.

Chapter 19:   "Lifesong," Casting Crowns, 2005.
"What Faith Can Do," Kutless, 2009

Chapter 20:   "At the Cross," Hillsong United, 2006.

Chapter 22:   "Let the Waters Rise," Mikeschair, 2010.

Chapter 23:   "Let the Peace of God Reign," Darlene Zschech, 1996.

Chapter 24:   "I Will Rise," Chris Tomlin, 2008.

Chapter 25:   "If We Are The Body," Casting Crowns, 2003

Chapter 26:   "Hear Us From Heaven," Jared Anderson, Vertical Worship Songs, 2004.

Chapter 27:   "What Do I Know of Holy?" Addison Road, 2008.

Chapter 29:   "Show Me Your Glory," Third Day, 2003.

Breinigsville, PA USA
25 January 2011
254064BV00002B/2/P